CROSSING THE HALL

Exposing an American Divide

By Lori Wojtowicz

Print Edition

ISBN: 978-1-7337810-0-8

Author's Photo by G.E. Anderson

She remembered the little white robe and hood,

just like her father's.

CONTENTS

WITH GRATITUDE...

WHEN I STAND IN FRONT of a classroom, students think I am *the* teacher. What they don't see are all the teachers who taught me. Stan Bidlack, Richard Ballard, and Denise Eaddy-Richardson, your presence is always with me. You are my mentors whose inspiration, intuition, and intelligence continue to challenge me to be a better educator.

I thank Dolores Turner, Krystal Abney, Kay Wade, Noel Folks, Byron Douglas, and Brother Umar for opening my eyes; Sarah Andrew Vaughn for helping me to write; Maryan Mastey and Carey Culbertson for your enduring friendship; Georgia Donovan for her belief in creativity; and all the others who know who they are.

And to my daughters, Jessica, Tara, and Rachal, thank you for your very existence. To say I am proud of you and what you contribute to the world is an understatement. You may be surprised to know how much I want you to be proud of me.

Finally and forever, thank you Phil. Your belief in me is unwavering.

PREFACE

SOMEONE ONCE ASKED ME to describe my culture, and I searched for words. It actually didn't feel like I had one, but I didn't want to admit that so I talked about my Scotch-Irish heritage even though I barely know anything about it. Bagpipes? Potatoes? Four leaf clovers? But the person shook their head, no. "Describe your white, Christian culture." Even with that focus I felt at a loss. The Christian part I could answer: "Church on Sundays, praying before meals, hoping for Heaven." The white part left me blank.

I think a lot of us living in The Land of Only White feel like this. It's all we've ever known so, ironically, it's hard to define. There's nothing juxtaposing it to help with a definition of contrast. Our whiteness is so pervasive it's almost invisible.

Now that I've traveled beyond the borders of that colorless world, two seemingly unconnected childhood memories surface: *The Wizard of Oz* and *Amazing Grace*.

The original film starring the young Judy Garland debuted in 1939, but in 1956 it reappeared in amazing Technicolor. I was one year old. For as far back as I can remember I waited for its yearly return on television, never missing it. Safely snuggled on my dad's lap was the perfect place to watch the Wicked Witch of the West and her terrifying flying monkeys. Even as an adult I have dragged my children to see numerous stage productions, and I know I have enjoyed them more than they did. I identify with Dorothy.

She longed for a land beyond her Kansas doorstep, a place "somewhere over the rainbow," and she traveled there. When she returned home, she told everyone of her adventures in The Land of Oz. And she was honest, telling them "some of it wasn't very nice." They attributed her words to a bad bump on her head, that she dreamed it all. Certainly this other land wasn't real. No one believed her.

Dorothy left home abruptly, dropped directly into another world. Leaving my home in The Land of Only White has been a longer trek. But when I try to tell my family about this other region I have seen, I know that they think I've suffered a bump on the head too, that I'm at least a bit delusional. Certainly, they know I'm not seeing clearly. They don't believe me.

And John Newton's hymn, *Amazing Grace,* reverberates through my entire life. I remember my father's deep baritone voice singing it in church, it was the music of my wedding, and the haunting sounds of a bagpipe moaned its melody at my father's funeral. I have already told my children to play it when they bury me. "I was lost, but now I'm found." These are the lyrics I love, but they no longer describe me. I'm still lost, and I am content with that.

This is the story of getting lost leaving The Land of Only White. An unlikely pair, Plato and Malcolm X (one white, one black, both dead), have served as guides imploring me to leave, to wander beyond its borders. So have my students. I thank them all.

SHADOWS

Time Served

"Pomp and Circumstance," chords from the orchestra fill the auditorium. Students in black robes file in, many somber and solemn, some unable to contain their joy. Many scan the audience looking for family, and when their eyes meet, both students and families cheer. Others look dazed, baffled that they have actually made it to their high school graduation. And a few look toasted, already well into the party that will follow. From my vantage point on stage, it is a scene I have watched replay annually for thirty-four years.

I am a teacher, and next year will be my last. I will walk free from the institution that has claimed my youth. Having grown old within its walls—entering in my twenties and leaving nearing sixty—I've served a life sentence.

I wonder as I do with each graduating class, where the students will go from here? What will their lives hold for them? Now I wonder where I will go when I, too, graduate into retirement. I have paced the cell of my classroom for over six thousand days, walking miles without going anywhere. But that's a lie. I am in a different land, far from where I began. I've gone somewhere. I know because I often feel lost.

When I began my teaching career, I was a new graduate myself. An alumna from a prestigious, private college, I was ready to teach. I was highly educated; in fact, I knew I was smart. There was proof: my diploma read *magna cum laude*, and

Phil Beta Kappa had taught me the secret handshake. I was ready to enrich the lives of students with my knowledge. And so in those early years of teaching, I watched my students walk across the stage to their futures feeling confident, certain I had educated them well. They were right to have placed their trust in me. But in recent years I have started each school year by writing on the board, "Don't trust your teachers." And I no longer sit on stage congratulating myself.

Let me tell you about two of my students. From childhood, both Debra and DeAndre knew they wanted to be veterinarians.

Debra, a white student, was in all accelerated classes and worked very hard. She did not work after school so she could concentrate on academics. When she was a junior, her parents sent her to a summer program for prospective vet students at a renowned university. In her senior year, the family agreed to take on a puppy that Debra wanted to train as a service-dog. Max, the black lab, occasionally came to class with her. She took SAT prep classes, was a member of National Honor Society, volunteered in the community, and played in the orchestra. Her parents paid for her college. She graduated near the top of her class and went on to graduate school at one of the best vet schools in the country. She is a vet today.

DeAndre, an African American student, was in my first-hour class, and he was always there before me. He came to school early, got his free breakfast, and headed to the quiet classroom to finish homework. He was not in all accelerated classes, and he worked very hard. He balanced school with part-time jobs to help supplement his mother's income. They moved frequently; employment came and went. He couldn't afford a dog or an SAT prep class. He wrote poetry, participated in citywide poetry performances, and volunteered at a vet clinic. Money for college was a real concern; his family needed him to stay home to help them survive. He went away to a university, but found it too difficult to balance academics, finances, and family pressures. He left the university and enrolled in a community college vet-tech program. He is doing very well and will graduate in a year.

I asked both why they wanted to be veterinarians. Debra talked of her early love of animals and her love of science later. DeAndre talked of his childhood in Detroit, of witnessing men gambling on dog fighting, and watching the maimed animals being discarded in trashcans, of peering into the trashcans when no one was watching. He saw the dying dogs and knew one day he would help them. And he will. So will Debra.

Debra and DeAndre shared the same dream, but their paths were very different. Outside the classroom, Debra had lots of support, a stable family, and ample finances. DeAndre had far less. Debra succeeded with the help of her circumstances; DeAndre in spite of them.

I am proud of both. They are success stories, but I no longer pat myself on the back for their accomplishments. They have come to represent the two populations I now teach in my high school. For years, I only taught those who looked like Debra.

THE LAND OF ONLY WHITE

WALKING IN FRONT OF A new class each September always brings a mixture of excitement and fear. Every kind of student sits there: the shy and reticent, the bold and brash. Some acknowledge your entrance; some ignore. But when I write "Don't trust your teachers" across the board before I speak, there is a spark of interest. Sometimes disbelief.

Then I write the rules. I used to have a lot of them—so many one chalkboard couldn't have contained them. Over the years they have dwindled to only four:

Read Critically

Think Deeply

Write Well

Act Wisely

I can't take credit for them. Another educator created them when he grew tired of all the rules school administration produced for students: "No hats, no food, no cell phones, no being tardy, no talking, no disrespect." He said we should start telling students what we wanted from them instead of what we didn't. His rules have governed my classroom for years, but it took me a very long time to hold myself to these same expectations.

Consider the first two. Almost all of my students can read,

but to *read critically* is a skill requiring constant practice and refinement. It means investing yourself in searching for meaning—your own meaning, not one neatly provided by the teacher, or *Spark Notes*, or the Internet. It takes work, requiring you to *think deeply*.

Since I start and end the year with Plato, students better be ready to apply those first two rules.

In 400 BC, Plato wrote "The Simile of the Cave."[1] He describes men who are chained deep within the earth. Shackled below since birth, they see only shadows of the world beyond. But they do not see themselves as prisoners. Their limited view has been their only reality. They live their lives oblivious of a world beyond their own, without vision beyond their narrow scope of existence. Plato writes that it takes someone from the outside world, an enlightened one, to free them from their ignorance and bring them into the light. Coming into the sun, into knowledge, can be painful. Many choose to remain within the comforting darkness of the cave.

Year after year, I taught this allegory feeling Plato would be pleased with me. I would not have admitted it, but I used to be sure I was, as Plato deemed them, one of the enlightened ones. After all, I was a teacher lifting my students out of their ignorance. But somewhere in those years that certainty faded. So many certainties have crumbled.

I know now that I have been a cave dweller. I might still be, but I do know there is something worth seeing beyond the darkness I used to live within. My cave, my comfort, and my certainties came from the land I was raised in, The Land of Only White.

Where is this land? Anywhere in America where the residents reside solely or predominantly with members of their own white race. It is a colorless world. When I write of it, forgive my generalizations. I am aware of them, drawing only on my experience, but I am confident many will know it as the land in which they, too, dwell. At least several aspects will align with home. For others, there may be only a few similarities. In all its variations, I know it still exists in America today.

When you are raised in The Land of Only White, one thing you know for sure is you are not a racist. The rhetoric of your childhood confirms it. Each weekday in school, I recited the Pledge of Allegiance, vowing "liberty and justice for all." And every Sunday my Christian church proclaimed the brotherhood of man. The minister's sermon, predictably repetitive, told us to "love our brother." We memorized and mouthed the message. We sang it in hymns: "Red and yellow, black and white. They are precious in his sight. Jesus loves the little children of the world."[2] I learned skin color didn't matter; in fact, I patted myself on the back for not even "seeing" color. We do that in The Land of Only White.

This was the cave I was raised within. These were the shadows on the wall I trusted, believed, and never doubted. And for a while, nothing disturbed my view.

Given this upbringing, it is no surprise that when I began teaching in a diverse high school, I also believed in the public school's promise of an "equal education for all." I might have been a new teacher, but with my impressive credentials it wasn't long before I was teaching Honors English, a course designed for highly motivated juniors. Although the high school's student body was racially diverse, honors classes were not. Mostly white faces from affluent families stared at me. I did not question why. They represented my own white and wealthy upbringing; I was comfortable and confident.

And then my schedule changed to include teaching African American Literature to predominantly African American students. The classrooms were separated by only a small span of hallway.

In his short story "The Man Who Killed a Shadow," Richard Wright describes that while black and white people often live in close proximity, the distance between them is actually vast, being separated by thousands of "psychological miles."[3] When I crossed that hallway between the Honors English and African American Literature classrooms, I had no idea how far from home I was traveling or how disorienting it would be. I got lost because I was being booted out of Plato's cave.

"DO YOU REALLY BELIEVE ALL STUDENTS CAN LEARN?"

BEFORE I BEGAN TEACHING African American Literature, I knew of the achievement gap, in particular, the disparity between high-achieving white students and lower-achieving African American students. It just hadn't been my problem. The gap didn't pertain to my white students in Honors English, except to confirm that most of them were exceptional students; therefore, I was probably an exceptional teacher. Now I taught black students and could not dismiss the disparity. If my excelling white students stood as evidence of my excellence, what did this achievement gap now say about me as an educator?

And how was I to hold on to my belief of equal education for all? I had been teaching for ten years, proud of working in a high school that prided itself in not "tracking" students into academic levels. Students were free to take whatever course they wanted, but their "choices" perpetuated a pattern, a system was established that assured the achievement gap's survival. Nearly 18% of the school's population was African American, but for years, the only diversity I saw was in the hallways, not in my classroom. Who taught the black students?

It took a colleague to point out that, in truth, our high school contained two separate schools: one for children held in high regard; one for children held in low regard. In this de facto segregation, white students filled the rigorous, upper-level courses; disproportionate numbers of black students filled the regular and lower level classes. I had been teaching in the first school; I entered the second when I crossed the hall.

"Do you really believe all students can learn?" The principal of my school often begins faculty meetings with this question. It seems rhetorical for educators, so easy to answer in the affirmative. She never seems to believe our assertion and never tires of asking the question. The teaching staff at my high school is predominantly white. She is black. Having spent forty years in education, it didn't take her ten years into her career to consider the achievement gap as it had for me. She has confronted it always. She knows it lives, breathes, and continues to determine and destroy students' lives. It could have claimed her own.

She formed plenty of committees over the years to confront and close the gap; I joined many. They produced talk that took no action, talk that turned to silence as soon as the meeting ended. I think my principal knew all along what the problem was. Time on a committee was wasted if individuals hadn't prepared in honest, sometimes painful, personal contemplation. I think that is why she asked her question so often: "Do you *really* believe all students can learn?"

She asked teachers to reflect on our own upbringing and the "racial" education we had received. I remember thinking, "Reflect on *what*?" If you believe your racial upbringing has been colorless, what is there to see?

But I actually do remember the first time I saw a black person.

I was in the third grade and living in an apartment while we looked for a new home. The complex provided a babysitting service, and one evening my parents decided to call for a sitter. A dinner party, I remember them dressed up, ready to go. The door opened to a young black woman. Even now I can remember how dark she was. She smiled at me, and I kissed my parents good-bye.

They were home in twenty minutes. I don't know what reason they gave the babysitter. When she had gone, they questioned if I was all right, and then said that they just hadn't realized she would be "a Negro." No one said she was bad or dangerous, just the words, "We didn't realize she would be a Negro."

The shadows of my cave taught me skin color didn't matter. That was the overt message. But my parents were also schooling me on race when they refused to go to a dinner party because they had left their child in the care, or danger, of a black woman. Thus began my double-sided racial curriculum, a covert education veiled beneath the overt. The shadows were beginning to fade.

THE ISLAND

AUTHORS, ARTISTS, AND PHILOSOPHERS of all times have explored Plato's allegory of enlightenment. Films of my generation are no exception. It may be a stretch from Plato to current day comedian and actor Jim Carrey, but the connection is there nonetheless. Jim Carrey starred in the 1998 movie, *The Truman Show*. I use the film in class to put a modern-day spin on Plato's theme. Students love it.

Jim Carrey plays the role of Truman Burbank, a man living a lovely life on an island in the town of Sea Haven. What Truman doesn't realize is that he is the *only* star of a reality television show, broadcast twenty-four hours a day to the public. Sea Haven is an elaborately constructed and contained television set. All the residents are paid actors who participate in Truman's deception, even his wife. He is a prisoner; Sea Haven is the equivalent of Plato's cave. Truman believes he is free, unaware of a corporation's total control of his life. Through the staged comforts of his existence and a conditioned fear of water, the director is confident that Truman will never leave, stating, "We all accept the reality we are presented." Like the men in Plato's cave, Truman is unaware of his chains, his ignorance of a world beyond his own.

Here is the enduring message. We are all Trumans. We accept the assumptions and conventions of our upbringing, controlled initially by those who raise us and later by the society that shapes us. Plato says we need an enlightened one from beyond our boundaries to help expand our vision and our knowledge.

Just like my students, I loved watching *The Truman Show.* For me it held not only allegorical meaning, but literal as well. I spent a part of my youth on Mercer Island, an upscale suburban community of Seattle, Washington. It was a kind of Sea Haven: comforts, country clubs, and Sundays at church. It was primarily an island of white: nearly 80 percent, with Asians making up another 15 percent. African Americans comprised only about 1 percent. I do not believe my parents had any conscious racist intentions in moving there. Living on Mercer Island symbolized success. The median income for families was well over twice the rest of the country. It just happened to be nearly all white. No one I knew questioned why.

Racism didn't seem to exist on my island. How could you be a racist in The Land of Only White? The church's commandment to "Love thy neighbor as thyself," was easy: all my neighbors looked just like me. I never thought if that rule extended to the land over the bridge. I was taught to love one another; there just weren't any *others.*

And Plato would say that's the problem. It takes someone from beyond the boundaries to expand one's vision, someone who makes you question how accurate your perception and beliefs actually are. For the men in the cave, it was an enlightened one. For Truman, it was a woman from beyond the set who helped him see past his imprisonment.

For me, it began with Malcolm X.

With the exception of the black babysitter's short stay, the only black people who made it into my childhood home were on television. In the early 1960s, that meant Martin Luther King, Jr. A man of non-violence, he talked of peaceful, patient integration. He spoke the language of our Christian Church, dreaming that one day "little black boys and black girls will be able to join hands with little white boys and white girls as sisters and brothers."[4] He dreamed, but in reality nothing changed in my neighborhood, and the only hands I held were white. My parents liked Martin. He was "a good Negro."

But there was another—tall, slight of build, and wearing glasses—that the media succeeded in making into a menacing man of hate: Malcolm X. My parents believed the media's message. He was "a bad Negro."

Malcolm X wasn't patient, and at that time, he didn't want integration. He wanted separation, Black Nationalism, for black communities to be self-sufficient and removed from White America. He was reviled by White America for his militant views cloaked in violent rhetoric.

Violent language was considered uncouth and ill mannered in my Land of Only White, but ironically, I now realize my parents were in complete agreement with Malcolm X. Just like him, they preached self-reliance and independence. And just like him, they wanted separation: white neighborhoods, white schools, and white babysitters for white children. Our church may have said we should love our brother, but the covert message was to love the darker brothers only from a very safe distance far over the bridge.

White America accepted Martin Luther King, Jr. But Malcolm X was, as civil rights activist and actor Ozzie Davis once described him, "the outsider," the "other brother," rebuked and feared.[5] I'm not sure if Plato would have seen Malcolm X as an enlightened one, but he certainly was an "other" in my world. I had accepted the messages I received on Malcolm X in my childhood: he was a bad man of hate. But when I began teaching African American Literature and read his words myself, I found a profound contradiction.

Malcolm X's message was not one of violence, but of education.

The writings of Malcolm X challenged my previous understanding of racism in America. Before, I believed racism existed only in individual events that were easily identified. Slavery was racist: it existed in the past and was long since over. The KKK was a group of racist people: thank goodness they didn't live on my island. The 1963 bombings of Birmingham that killed four little black girls attending Sunday school were racist: we didn't have black churches and Alabama was far away in the South. Like stains on a cloth, racism was easily identifiable.

And I was clean.

Malcolm said racism was more than an obvious blemish. It was a thread entwined in the very fabric of our country. This was a *system* of racism, an American system of power and oppression.

And I was not exempt.

As an English teacher, I am familiar with the theme of power and its potential to corrupt. I can lecture on the misuse of political power in 11th century Scotland portrayed in Shakespeare's *Macbeth*; 17th century Boston's Puritanical control described in Hawthorne's *The Scarlet Letter*; the dictatorships of dystopian societies in Huxley's *Brave New World* and Orwell's *1984*; and even Nurse Ratched's psychological domination over patients in a 20th century mental institution in Ken Kesey's *One Flew Over the Cuckoo's Nest.* My white students enjoy these texts and the rich debates they bring. As long as we were talking about someplace and someone else, considering power and oppression is just fine.

But two other required texts, Twain's *The Adventures of Huckleberry Finn* and Wright's *Native Son*, often elicit a different reaction from some white students, one of reluctance and even outright resistance. As one told me, "Oh no, not again. We already know this 'race' stuff. We did it last year." And in truth, before Malcolm X, I thought I had already done race also. Twain and Wright wrote about an old America, not my America. I had nothing left to learn or consider. Nothing to see, especially not in myself.

Sometimes I think that's what we teachers do best: examine, dissect, and judge subjects other than ourselves. It was Plato's teacher, Socrates, who said, "The unexamined life is not worth living."[6] How many times had I taught that line to students without applying it to myself?

Before you can consider leaving whatever cave claims you, you have to examine the chains of your own ignorance. And here was Malcolm X asking me to consider my place in a system of power and oppression based on race in my country, my classroom, and in my home.

I needed a definition to begin. Almost everything I read described a system of power and oppression in similar terms:

Those who are in power create and organize struc-

> tures, institutions, and policies so that those who are in power will remain in power. Those who are powerless must struggle against a sometimes invisible system which is designed to keep them powerless. This is a system of oppression.[7]

If such a system existed, it certainly wasn't visible to me. I didn't even believe it. I was white, but I sure hadn't created or organized anything as substantial as a structure, or institution, or policy. In fact, I lived in structures, worked in an institution, and followed policies—all created by someone else. I certainly didn't feel powerful. But here was Malcolm X asking me not to turn away, to consider rather than to dismiss. He asked me to see through an *other's* eyes.

A New Language

Plato's prisoners didn't know they were chained. It's kind of like living on an island. Unless you live by the bridge, you can forget that there are boundaries. You know your land so well, and it is enough. I knew this to be true from living on Mercer Island. Everything we needed was there: stores, schools, churches. You didn't have to leave the island unless you chose to. You had to make a conscious decision to go.

I think many people from The Land of Only White want to stay put.

Malcolm X's concept of a system of racism was forcing me over the bridge and into unknown territory. Like traveling abroad, I needed to learn a new language. Preparing to teach African American Literature immersed me in the study of African American history. This was not the United States history I had been taught. Here I learned the language of *power and oppression.* Not my native vernacular, the words helped me see another America that had been obscured by the shadows of my upbringing.

Five terms repeatedly appeared in my reading, and all were new to me: overt and covert racism; institutional and internalized racism; conferred dominance. These concepts opened up an avenue to help me navigate my own past, exposing a racial education I thought had not existed. I had been schooled well, taught to remain blind.

The first is the most obvious: *overt racism*. This is open racism with the intent to harm. It's easy to distinguish and easy to condemn. Even those of us raised in The Land of Only White can spot it. Slavery and the Jim Crow Era, we're pretty sure overt racism existed only in the past. These are the stains on our history, but in our present they have been washed away. If anything, the past reassures us of all the progress we've made. We can be proud. Before I read Malcolm X, this had been the sum total of my understanding of race in America. I didn't really see overt racism anymore, but I understood the term.

But the second haunted me: *covert racism*. This is undercover racism, sometimes without intent to harm. The racist may not even be aware he is a racist.

The racist may not even be aware. No intent to harm. My parents and the black babysitter. They had no desire to harm her. They didn't insult her. They just couldn't leave their child alone with her. And they would have told you they weren't racist.

More memories surfaced giving illustration and validity to the term.

Many years ago an old friend's sixteen-year-old daughter wanted to watch me teach. She was considering being a teacher. "Got any guys in your class I'd like?" she queried on the drive to the high school. "Guys you think I'd like to hang with?"

I realized she wasn't just coming to see me or consider a career choice, and I had to think over my students in a new light. Sure, I could picture some guys for her, and so we designed our plan. At the beginning of each class I would get students involved in a discussion. When my *choice* for her raised his hand, I would look in her direction with a subtle grin. It seemed harmless until I sent my smile sailing during the first class. She looked back at me in revulsion. When the class ended, I found out why:

"I thought we were only looking at the white guys."

Covert racism. She had no intent to harm. She assumed we shared that understanding, assumed we would only see white. All other males just didn't exist.

We did share the same background firmly rooted in The Land of Only White, so I really shouldn't have been surprised by her reaction. She attended the same high school as her mother and me had; our families had been members of the same church. One difference I remembered was that in my old friend's home racial jokes were commonplace. There was a lot of laughter. Harmless humor at the expensive of no one, and they were good church-going people—certainly not racist.

I think my old friend and her daughter laughed at the jokes...and learned.

We shared some of the rarely spoken, but nevertheless understood codes of our upbringing. While the minister preached, and it was echoed in our home, that we were all the same regardless of skin color, cloaked there also was the quiet message that blacks were to be avoided, never dated, and marriage between races was just plain wrong. I don't remember even learning the latter. Overtly, clearly we were not racist. Covertly, well, you just didn't talk about this. For a very long time, I didn't even see the contradiction.

We didn't "see" color, except when we did.

The message to avoid African Americans had a subtext. Don't only avoid them—fear them. It's easy to fear what you don't know. When you live on an island, everything over the bridge can look dark and dangerous.

LEARNING FEAR

MY MOTHER WOULD NEVER HAVE ADMITTED fearing African Americans, but I think of a hot, summer day several years ago. I lived near a middle school. My then seventy-some year old mother had come to visit. We sat at the kitchen table near the screen door, trying to catch a breeze. Summer school was being dismissed for the day. Young teens, many of them black, walked by the open door. My mother got up, closed the door, and locked it. When I asked why, she told me, "I got a chill." It was a hot, humid day, and she had gotten a chill. I don't know that she could have identified it, but I know a shiver of fear had blown through her.

Black students tell me that they know many white people lock their car doors when they walk by; they can add my mother to their list. I think back to the black babysitter and the terror that brought my parents home. And I think of just a couple of years ago when my daughter got married in downtown Detroit. Without ever speaking of race, some of my relatives worried that it would be too dangerous and just stayed home. Others came, and were surprised they lived to tell about it.

I also think of Ben, a student in Honors English. He designed a project to explore his "social web." Constructing an intricate visual representation, he created a structure of yarn with pictures of his friends caught within. His intent was to show the racial and cultural diversity of his respected peers, but his completed sculpture disturbed him. White faces looked back at him. Two black faces gazed at him also, but he was honest enough to know they were only acquaintances he had included to make himself look good, to get an "A." He believed his web would celebrate the diversity of his friendships. Instead, his prejudice stared at him.

Begun in the safety of his comfort zone, the completed project led him over the bridge into the uncomfortable. Ben admitted he was afraid of most black students. He didn't know where this fear had taken hold, but its grip was strong. Thinking back, he could find no event that would have given validity to his apprehension. No scary black person lurked in his past; in fact, there were almost no interactions. Few, if any, African American students sat in his honors classes. Encounters with black students in his *diverse* high school were relegated to the hallways. There he just tried to stay clear of them.

Ben's contemplations began to center on the media. He remembered hours in front of the television and in movie theaters that had exposed him to a common character: the black criminal. In his adolescence, music videos further schooled him on black males. Rough, tough, and uninhibited by social constraints, they always had guns. They demanded you fear them. Without realizing it, Ben believed he projected these images onto the black students he saw in the school halls. The media had infiltrated his mind, and it was safer to keep walking past these students than get to know them.

For good and bad, the media does educate. Sometimes the lessons are overt and accurate; sometimes subliminal and false. We, the audience, don't always critically evaluate the messages. In The Land of Only White, without actual contact or interactions, fearful black stereotypes can be ingested and accepted as reality, even without actual evidence.

Ben had "learned" avoidance and fear. Unaware, the teachings on race had determined where he would find friendship. Many of us in The Land of Only White are like Ben. We might not realize we are being schooled, but we, too, have learned this covert racial education of avoidance and fear.

Ben had begun to uncover the subliminal, but what about those of us who don't? I wonder how this undercover education plays out for white teachers who stand in front of diverse classrooms?

Many black students believe white teachers are often afraid of them. Their evidence? Teachers who find a way to remain at a safe distance, barricaded behind a desk or podium instead of moving freely through rows of desks; those who never smile or laugh but avoid eye contact at all costs; those who call for an assistant principal to escort a black student out of the classroom rather than talk face-to-face about a conflict.

Some teachers just try to avoid black students completely; so, just like my cousin, they don't "see" them: they don't call on a raised hand, they write bathroom passes to allow students to leave class and don't care how long it takes for them to return, they don't expect anything from them. Tanya, an African American student in her junior year, told me she knew her white teacher didn't know her name at the conclusion of the school year.

Sometimes, when the students see they have become invisible, they request a transfer to another class. Sometimes, they just sit there and are promoted to the next grade for doing nearly nothing. And some just stop coming. Then teachers lament, "How can I teach *those* students if they aren't in my class?" without considering their hand in eliminating them. Actually, they've "taught" them a great deal. Students feel unwelcomed in their own school, locked out of an educational system that grants others recognition and academic success. Avoidance and fear are hard to identify in yourself. But it is easy to get rid of black students who sit in your class.

Sometimes, it's the students who get rid of a teacher.

I remember being summoned to a classroom where a white substitute teacher and a group of black students were in a shouting match. Tempers were hot on both sides; teacher and students wanted to be heard. In the privacy of the hall, the woman told me of her anger at *those* students, that she "knew their kind." She was sure I understood what she meant…and I did. Her anger clearly masked fear. She had been outnumbered by *those students*. She may have thought not identifying them as black students kept her from being a racist, but her assumption that as a white woman I would share her view only confirmed it. The school day was nearly over; I told her to go home.

When I returned to the classroom, students told me that the lady hated them. One student offered smugly, "I don't think she has much teaching potential." I silently agreed.

The students saw a racist and stood up to her, but I wonder now about the covert racism of fear that lives in many of us from The Land of Only White, buried but still present. How does it color (and I use that term with intention) our teaching?

From Fear to Inferiority

Malcolm X introduced me to the concept of systemic racism in our country. Civil rights activist and author Michelle Alexander furthered my vision in her book *The New Jim Crow* (2010). She describes "structural racism," using Iris Marion Young's metaphor of a birdcage to help visualize its control:

> If one thinks about racism by examining only one wire of the cage, or one form of disadvantage, it is difficult to understand how and why the bird is trapped. Only a large number of wires arranged in a specific way, and connected to one another, serve to enclose the bird and to ensure that it cannot escape....What is particularly important to keep in mind is that any given wire of the cage may or may not be specifically developed for the purpose of trapping the bird, yet it still cooperates (together with the other wires) to restrict its freedom.[8]

This image illustrates the third term in the language of power and oppression: *institutional racism.* Definitions vary, but most concur that institutional racism is the mistreatment of a particular group of people sustained by laws, customs, and practices that produce inequities. The mistreatment becomes so much a part of the society that it is often difficult to see the oppression, especially by those who are not the targeted group.[9]

No wonder we, in The Land of Only White, don't think we're racist. We really don't see it. We don't see the intricate societal design that holds the system in place. We don't see our hand in the blueprints. Consider the birdcage: those who help maintain its structure may not be familiar with every wire in the elaborate construction. Even the bird may be blind to all the elements that bind him. But if that bird begins to believe he deserves to be caged, then he has internalized the institutional message of inequality. He sees himself as less than those who live outside the wires. This is *internalized racism.*

I was lost in all this new terminology, lost in a land far from my own experience. I didn't know if I really believed any of it. And then my daughter helped me see.

"How do blonde brain cells die?" *Alone.*

"What do UFOs and smart blondes have in common?" *You hear about them all the time, but you never see one.*

"Why does it take longer to build a blonde snowman?" *Cause you have to hollow out its head.*

Over dinner, my daughter spilled out every blonde joke she had heard that day in her third grade class. She was the excited entertainer, we her all-blonde audience. Each joke confirmed the stupidity of blonde females, and her own gold curls bounced with laughter. But after, as I stood doing the dishes, she tugged at my arm. "I gotta ask you something." Her eyes were large and intent. "Are they true?"

Puzzled, I asked, "Are what true?"

"The jokes," she said. "Are we really dumber?"

Jokes don't mean anything. Don't take things too seriously. I hear this all the time, and I agree. It's good to laugh, and the intent of dumb blonde jokes is certainly humor, not harm. But my child feared these innocuous jokes might hold some truth. She had begun to doubt her own intelligence.

I could easily reassure her. Nothing else in her environment contributed to the correlation between blonde hair and lack of brainpower. Her teachers told her she was smart, she knew many professional women who were blondes, and I think she believed her own blonde mother was smart enough. She trusted my answer. They were simply jokes. It was fine to laugh. She relaxed, blonde and intelligent. But what if the message about stupidity did not come from a harmless joke? What if the environment bombarded her with messages, both overt and covert, of her own inferiority? When there is a societal confirmation that you are less, it takes more than a mother's voice to counteract it.

It is hard to envision America's collective voice teaching children to devalue themselves, but Dr. Kenneth Clark and his wife, Mamie, brought this reality to consciousness in their famous doll studies of the 1940s. Their work surfaced the destructive power of an institutionalized message of inferiority on black children's self-esteem.

Given a choice between two dolls identical except for race, African American children between the ages of six and nine were asked to identify the "nice" doll and the one they "liked best." The majority chose the white doll. They were then asked which was the "bad" doll, and the majority chose the black doll. When asked which doll looked most like them, some of the African American children who had identified the black doll as "bad" refused to answer or started crying. Clark concluded, "Prejudice, discrimination, and segregation from the society at large caused many black children to develop a sense of inferiority and self-hatred."[10] At a very young age, society's message had been implanted. Institutional racism became internalized.

This is teaching self-hate.

The children in Clark's study saw themselves as inferior, but I don't believe they could have articulated where they learned this. When a belief is institutionalized, it just is. It takes root in our core. Even when laws change, the beliefs fester.

Kenneth Clark's doll studies aided the Supreme Court's decision to end segregation in the 1954 *Brown v Board of Education* case. Black children may have had legal access to classrooms, but often still saw themselves as less. A law is only one wire in the birdcage. Remove it and the bird still remains trapped by a multitude of other barriers reminding it that it cannot fly. The passage of time doesn't necessarily weaken the cage.

Activist Kira Davis repeated the doll study with little girls in Harlem in 2005. Instead of showing an improved self-image, the results mirrored Clark's findings.[11] In 2010, CNN's Anderson Cooper conducted a similar study. When shown a range of skin tones from dark brown to very white, an African American boy was asked what skin color he wanted. He immediately pointed to the whitest shade. When asked why, he replied, "Because...I don't know why." A little African American girl pointed to the second lightest, explaining as she pointed to her own skin, "Because it's lighter than this. I don't like the way brown looks...it looks nasty for some reason."[12] Margaret Beale Spencer, child psychologist and professor at the University of Chicago, reflected on this study, commenting that even in 2010, "We are still living in a society where dark things are devalued and white things are valued."[13]

But I don't need to read studies. These children from the research represent the teenagers in my classroom today. I think of African American girls who have told me they will only marry someone "light skinned" in the hopes of having "light-skinned" babies or turning on each other because the "light-skinned ones always think they're better." I hear conversations about "good hair" if it is straight like whites, or of another who remembers her grandmother smearing her dark skin with bleaching cream to help make her pretty. I think of intelligent African American students who will not enroll in rigorous academic courses because "those are only for whites." They believe they are not smart enough. They have internalized an institutional message of self-hate. They sit in classrooms today.

America's overt, historical messages of African American inferiority are easy to trace. As early as the mid 1600s, African Americans held in slavery were told they were of no more value than cattle. The status "improved" in 1787 when the government told them they were now worth three-fifths of a person in the Three-Fifths Compromise between Northern and Southern states. The Jim Crow Era lasted from the end of the Civil War through the Civil Rights Movement of the 1960s. Under the thin veil of "separate but equal," Jim Crow Laws insured that whites would remain in power in every arena. From where you went to the bathroom to where you were buried, Jim Crow reduced African Americans' lives to subservience.

Malcolm X saw the injustice of these overt laws but feared

more the insidious danger of internalized racism. He wrote, "America's greatest crime against the black man was not slavery or lynching, but that he was taught to wear a mask of self-hate and self-doubt."[14]

When everything in your environment demeans you, how do you deny its entry into your psyche? Perhaps Joseph Goebbel, Hitler's horrific propaganda minister, said it best: "If you tell a lie big enough and keep repeating it, people will eventually come to believe it."[15]

America lied to African Americans. The effect of those historic lies live on.

In The Land of Only White we want to believe the Civil Rights Movement of the 1960s changed it all. "Yes, things were bad, but now they're better. Now they're fair." I hear this all the time. If this were true why is it more African American adults are under correctional control today—in prison or jail, on probation or parole—than were enslaved in 1850?[16] Why are schools more racially segregated now than in the 1960s?[17] And why is there an achievement gap that continues to ensure who will prosper and who will not? Why is it just this year a colleague shared her young daughter's proclamation, "I just don't want to be brown anymore"? In schools across America, I wonder what we are teaching African American students they are? Why do so many leave education behind? Are we exposing the institutional lie of inferiority or allowing them to remain in a cave of self-doubt? Aren't they shackled, just like the prisoners of Plato's cave, seeing only the distorted shadows of their true selves?

Of course, the question we white teachers should ask is if we believe the lie ourselves.

Malcolm X's white teacher told him that he was a *nigger.* One of the brightest in his 8th grade class, his teacher questioned him on his future plans. Malcolm responded that he'd been thinking about becoming a lawyer and never forgot his instructor's reaction. "He kind of half smiled and said, 'Malcolm, one of life's first needs is for us to be realistic. Don't misunderstand me, now. We all here like you, you know that. But you've got to be realistic about being a nigger. A lawyer—that's no realistic goal for a nigger. You need to think about something you can be.'"[18]

Malcolm left school that year. In his autobiography, he tries to explain his exit from education:

> What makes the ghetto hustler yet more dangerous is his "glamour" image to the school-dropout youth in the ghetto. These ghetto teenagers see the hell caught by their parents struggling to get somewhere, or see that they have given up struggling in the prejudiced, intolerant white man's world. The ghetto teen-agers make up their own minds they would rather be like the hustlers whom they see dressed "sharp" and flashing money and displaying no respect for anybody or anything. So the ghetto youth become attracted to the hustler worlds of dope, thievery, prostitution, and general crime and immorality.[19]

Malcolm X's words are echoed by current day author and *Washington Post* reporter, Nathan McCall, in his piece, "Dispatches from a Dying Generation" (1991). He writes of his own high school experience in the 1970s, that expanded beyond the "ghetto youth," to encompass his own black middle class upbringing. While he acknowledges that there were good role models of black success, they were unable to positively influence McCall or his peers. He writes:

> They were unappealing to us as heroes. They couldn't stand up to the white man. They didn't fulfill our notions about manhood. Instead, we revered the guys on the streets, the thugs who were brazen and belligerent …they shunned the white establishment and worshipped violence. In our eyes, they were real men. We studied their bouncy walk and the slick, lyrical way they talked.

McCall continues, "The concept of education as a passport to a better life was vague to us. We saw no relation between school and our reality. That's why it was so easy for my buddies to drop out in our sophomore year."[20]

Malcolm left school in the 8th grade. McCall's peers left in the 10th. I see many black students today who last long enough to walk across a stage at graduation, but have left learning behind long ago. White students who excel academically are often perceived as nerds, and a nerd isn't cool. A nerd is, however, academically successful and praised for his intelligence. With the belief that education's power and possibility to change a life exists only for whites, many black students instead embrace an image of being cool. They adopt a "just get by" mentality, doing the bare minimum to pass, operating in survival mode in the classroom. They survive to graduation, but the future is often a dead end.

Of course, I do see some African American students who succeed academically, but it often comes at a price: ridicule and alienation from their own black peers. I have witnessed this first hand, far too often: an African American student completes a writing assignment. It is intelligent and insightful; I want to use it as a model of excellence for others. When I ask to share it with the class, sometimes the student refuses me completely; more often, he tells me that I may, as long as I keep his name off of it. I see the pride on the student's face that the excellence of the work has been acknowledged, but he must remain anonymous. To be acknowledged as a scholar would be to risk being ostracized, to be accused of acting "white."

This "burden of acting white" is a phenomenon anthropologist John Ogbu, Signithia Fordham, and others have studied. In 1986, Ogbu and Fordham wrote:

> When white Americans traditionally refuse to acknowledge that black Americans are capable of intellectual achievement…black Americans subsequently begin to doubt their own intellectual ability, begin to define academic success as white people's prerogative, and begin to discourage their peers, perhaps unconsciously, from emulating white people in academic striving. Consequently, many black students who are academically able do not put forth the necessary effort and perseverance in their schoolwork and do poorly in school."[21]

I think back to those children and the dolls. What if they

had been asked to pick the "smart" doll? I am sure the white one would have been chosen, so where does that leave the black doll, the black child?

What if the achievement gap persists because society's institutional and internalized message has become "white students are smart; black students are cool"? What if, at some buried level far below the surface, we white teachers believe it too.

Rashan was cool. He walked into my classroom straight from Chicago's inner city. Family issues brought him to my school a few weeks into the year. Brazen and bold, he held the glamour of the ghetto youth Malcolm X had written about. He had the "bouncy" walk and the "slick and lyrical" voice Nathan McCall described. Within minutes, he let us know we were lame; his world was filled with drugs, violence, and adrenaline.

The class was taking a required, standardized reading test when he made his entrance, and we did look rather lame. He mocked the test and me, refusing to take it. His brash behavior awed his audience. A few other students now felt brave enough to mumble complaints about the test. When I finally convinced him to try, he blew through it so he could continue to entertain. He held the spotlight.

His score was so low it was unrecognizable.

I knew Rashan was smart. I once had a professor tell me that he could pick out the bright students by the light in their eyes when he was lecturing. Educational experts now say we must be able to quantify the quality of a student. If you can't measure it and assign a number, it isn't real. My old professor would have been asked to rate the light in the eye on a scale of

1-10. I would have given Rashan a 9.5, and I trusted that glint in the eye more than the standardized reading test that would label him learning disabled.

There's a light that even bad behavior can't cloud. It's a light that wants to learn. Over the next few months, Rashan and I began to build a relationship of tentative trust. Some days I knew he was hustling me, a well practiced routine to prevent me from teaching and keep him in the spotlight. But there were moments when his innate hunger for learning forced him to drop his guard. Moments of brilliance and then a retreat back into the tough façade of disinterest. But the relationship continued. His skills many have been low, but his intellect was high. I was confident that the next reading test would reveal where his ability really was, and we would grow from there.

I was wrong. Rashan was more rude and unruly than on the first day. Worried other students would follow suit, I had to ask him to leave. Following him out into the hall, I felt like we were following some script that he had been playing and perfecting for a long time. He expected to be thrown out of class. He expected that I would lecture him, telling him his behavior would not be tolerated. He expected that I would throw him out for good. Mission accomplished. He had avoided the test. Instead, all I said was, "I know you're smart." I didn't know where I was going from there, and there was silence.

If Rashan had been thrown a bit off guard by my remark, I was knocked to the floor with his. He said, "That's the problem. If I take this test you'll find out you're wrong. You'll find out I'm not smart, and you won't like me anymore."

Rashan, this master of bravado, knew he was cool. He also believed that he was dumb.

I lost track of Rashan. Family issues again forced him to leave the school district. I wonder if he is still in school or has left for the streets. If he is in school, I wonder if he has finally been labeled learning disabled. I think there is a very good chance as a black male that he has. Nationwide, African American students comprise only 3 percent of the identified "gifted and talented" population, but 41 percent of the special education population.[22] Black and Hispanic males comprise 80 percent.[23]

Think about that term, *learning disabled.* If your society sends you an institutionalized message of academic inferiority, and you internalize it, surely that must count as a disability. Learning in the classroom is inevitably disabled when students do not believe they are capable.

Society's voice informs black students that they are less likely to graduate from high school than whites. It instructs black males that they are five times as likely to go to prison as college, and if they do make it to college, more than half will drop out. They are told they are more likely to be the victim of a violent crime.[24] They hear of an achievement gap, and know they reside at the bottom. Then we wonder why they don't try harder in school.

Jeron, a black student I had a few years back, poetically proclaimed: "All the hopes, the dreams I planted have not sprouted. How can they when statistics have them feeling crowded?" Jeron speaks from his own experience. Malcolm X spoke from his. He looked at a systemic failure in America that continues to produce generations of students with unfulfilled dreams.

Malcolm X wrote, "I have no compassion in me for a society that will crush a people, and then blame them for not being able to stand under the weight."[25] Many, especially those of us from The Land of Only White, will argue that there is no longer any weight crushing African Americans: the laws have changed, and dreams can be pursued.

And I agree. On the surface, opportunities abound, but below, a psychological lock is still being placed on the minds of many black students. By internalizing the messages of inferiority, many put the lock on themselves. If you don't believe the door of opportunity is for you, you won't work for the key; in fact, you won't even knock.

Think back to the men in Plato's cave. There are black students there who have sentenced themselves to sit in chains. Failing to believe in their innate potential and power, they are doomed to remain in darkness. But if those black students could but turn their heads, they would see that many of their white teachers, much of white America, sit shackled right beside them. We share the darkness.

In fact, we in The Land of Only White are often doubly blind. First, our sight is clouded by the derogatory stereotypes of African Americans that have taken hold within us. And second, we are blinded by a belief in our own superiority.

Plato and Malcolm X both wrote about deception. Plato penned, in the elegant language of a scholar, of the men in the cave: "In every way they would believe that the shadows of the objects…were the whole truth."[26]

Malcolm X spoke with blunt words of the street telling African Americans: "You've been hoodwinked. You've been had. You've been took. You've been led astray, lead amok. You've been bamboozled.[27]

Both men, writing two thousand years apart, believed deception needed to be confronted.

Malcolm X told African Americans to wake up, to see not only white America's chains, but also the chains of self-imprisonment. Deceived by a societal message of inferiority, he told them to face the truth and free themselves. We, in The Land of Only White, need to do the same. There's been a lot of bamboozling going on.

BAMBOOZLED BY SHIRLEY TEMPLE

SPIKE LEE'S FILM *Bamboozled* (2000), whose title stems directly from Malcolm X, has become part of my curriculum in African American Literature. Initially, I saw it as a black film appropriate for my black students. In his satirical creation, Lee examines the media's power, both past and present, to infiltrate the American audience's psyche, perpetuating a myth of black inferiority. He dissects the landscape of American film and television weaving in real images that give concrete proof of the derogatory African American stereotypes we all have been raised on. From the silent film, *Birth of a Nation* in 1915, to current day music videos of gangsta rappers, the black male is depicted as delinquent and dangerous. From *Amos and Andy*, originating in the 1920s to *Good Times* in the 70s, to Tyler Perry movies of today, African American adults are characterized as comedians, whose only value comes from making people laugh, at them. The common characterizations of deviant to buffoon expose the lie of inferiority I witnessed African American students ingesting. I felt *they* needed to see this film, and showed it year after year.

I think it was about my third viewing when I had a revelation, one I would be embarrassed to admit to Spike Lee: this was no *black* film for black audiences. This was an American film; its targeted audience was all of us. In the guise of entertainment, it wasn't just African Americans who were being subliminally educated on their inferiority. White Americans were being schooled also, doubly bamboozled by a myth of black inferiority and oh, yes—our own white superiority.

Remember Ben who came to believe the media had taught him to fear African Americans? Spike Lee exposed a subliminal curriculum on race that was far more pervasive. Fear and inferiority for African Americans. Superiority for whites. Americans, black and white, learned their lessons well.

Old film clips of Shirley Temple, the darling white child star of the 1930s and 40s appear in *Bamboozled.* The reruns of her movies were a part of my childhood, playing on my television every Saturday morning. Mesmerized by this precocious little white girl, I watched her tap-dance across my television screen. Shirley Temple, the entertainer, I did not see her as a teacher on race. But the movies' set often depicted a southern plantation, and she was the one with the brains, the mastermind in every plot. The black actors were relegated to play happy slaves and servants who danced, sang,—and obeyed her.

Shirley Temple, a harmless thread, not even a wire in the birdcage of systemic racism. Independently nothing at all, but consider that consistent message so much of the media sent: black inferiority and white superiority. Were any of us completely immune?

Another television series I never wanted to miss was *The White Shadow* (1978-1981). The show spotlighted a white coach who taught in an urban, black high school. He helped his students with everything. He wasn't just a good teacher; he was practically a saint.

The white savior—and in particular, the white savior-teacher—has been a media icon: *The Blackboard Jungle* (1955), *Dangerous Minds* (1995), and *The Freedom Writers* (2007) are but a few. All portray good white people who care. Those black kids would be lost without them. I love those films, but it's pretty clear to me now that white teachers aren't saving black students from anything. If we were, the achievement gap would have ceased to exist.

Many worry about the damaging effects of violence in the media, about the dangerous impact on children's susceptible, young minds. But what does the media's racial conditioning implant in children who grow into adults, some who find themselves as teachers in classrooms? Teachers believe that education is power, providing students the keys that unlock their own potential. What if, unaware and with the best of intention, we dole out those keys differently to white and black students based on our own buried racial assumptions?

Most teachers believe they hold high expectations for all students. September finds educators ebullient, but as the school year unfolds, reality erodes the ideal. Crowded classrooms, public criticism, long days that stretch into long nights of grading and preparations—teachers and high expectations get worn down.

Teachers forget their power, both for good and for bad. Their high expectations can help students attain goals they never thought possible; their low expectations can destroy confidence and dismantle self-worth. Most educators remember the Rosenthal-Jackson study (1968) from classes in college. We need to reread it. Rosenthal and Jackson questioned whether teacher expectations could actually raise IQ scores in students. They began by administering an IQ test to elementary students. The actual results were not shared. Instead, teachers were given the names of students who, based on the results, were expected to make the greatest gains in the classroom. In fact, these students were chosen at random. Their predicted growth had no basis in fact. At the end of the year, those students did indeed show the greatest academic gains. Rosenthal concluded that although teachers were unaware that they had treated them differently, implanting the mere suggestion that these children would be superior students was enough to change the teachers' interactions toward them. Without realizing it, teachers spent more time with these students, were more encouraging, and exposed them to more academically challenging tasks than the other students—simply because they believed in these children's academic abilities. Rosenthal labeled this self-fulfilling prophecy the Pygmalion Effect. His conclusion was powerful and succinct in its simplicity: students got smarter when teachers expected them to get smarter.[28]

The teachers in Rosenthal's study changed their behavior based on one bogus message, but we have been bombarded with countless negative racial messages. How do they inform our decisions in the classroom?

Some teachers actually acknowledge lowering expectations for black students. Without ill intent, they do so because they *care*. This kind of teacher just wants to help: help close the achievement gap, help students to pass to the next grade, help them walk across the stage at graduation. Walk across the stage to what? Protecting a student from rigorous academic demands, no matter one's intentions, only paralyzes the student's future. This kind of caring carries the assumption that black children are not as capable as white children; they need help in the form of lower expectations. I know these teachers because, for a while, I was one of them.

I cared enough to lie.

I let students believe that without much work or effort, they could be successful in my class, in college, and in careers. I pumped them up about the amazing futures awaiting them without being honest about the hard work and hardships required to bring dreams into reality. I think about one student in particular, Jadonna, who told me as she left my class that she was going to be a pediatrician. She was barely passing her other classes and had experienced her first "B" in mine. She believed it all possible.

I demanded little and promised much. Patting myself on the back for being a teacher who cared, I was proud that finally, in her senior year, Jadonna had a good school experience. I tried to silence the voice of truth in my head that knew she had neither the skills to get into college or the stamina to sustain it. Somewhere the reality of my lies confronted her. She works as a janitor now to support her family and still speaks of me fondly, but I know I failed her.

A Reflection

The notion that we, in The Land of Only White, hold a belief in our own superiority is not a pleasant one. It's easy to deny. I would have, but sometimes all it takes is a little reflection.

When my daughter was eight she stared into the bathroom mirror as I brushed her hair. She studied our reflection intently, blurting out, "We're white, right?" I had never heard her mention race. I nodded, yes.

"And we're better, right?"

It was a question, but its assertion staggered me. I had always believed in the color blindness of children; my own daughter destroyed that. I wanted someone to blame, and I chose her school. Having recently moved, I was confident that before this new location, she had never been exposed to anyone or anything that would have suggested this to her.

Phone calls to the elementary school principal and her teachers followed. They suggested other children must be repeating the rhetoric of their parents. We all wanted someone to blame for my child's misguided belief, but in reality, there was no individual villain. The culprit was a societal culture of whiteness that often contains a conscious, or not so conscious, belief in its own superiority. She spoke what she had learned.

It's hard to distill where this message of superiority comes from, and it isn't just the media. Consider the portraits of the all-white presidents that lined my daughter's classroom walls and had lined mine in elementary school decades before (though now the ratio would be forty-three white males to one black male, the message remains). It was reinforced by the nearly all white faces of her teachers. It was and continues to be proclaimed in the textbooks that celebrate white accomplishments and gloss over the less than stellar atrocities of slavery and more. Even Jesus and Santa still are nearly always depicted as white. Whiteness infiltrates all, but it's still hard to see. Kind of like air.

Dr. Beverly Tatum, psychologist and president of Spelman University, stated that this culture of white superiority is like "smog in the air. Sometimes it is so thick it is visible, other times it is less apparent, but always, day in and day out, we are breathing it in."[29] As the CNN investigation examining children's perceptions on race (2010) concluded, white children have an "overwhelming white bias" associating "their own skin with positive attributes and darker skin with negative attributes".[30] My daughter confirmed those findings.

I learned to say I didn't see color. It's what you do in The Land of Only White. But it's a lie. We see color; what we don't see is privilege.

THE PRIVILEGE OF IGNORANCE

ACTIVIST AND EDUCATOR PEGGY MCINTOSH, in her famous essay, "White Privilege: Unpacking the Invisible Knapsack," surfaces twenty-five ways whites are given advantages in this country that are often invisible to them.[31] From being a member of the racial majority, to being confident the legal system is working for and not against you—even knowing that flesh-colored bandages match your skin. You did not earn these advantages; they were bestowed upon you simply by being born white. And here is the final term in the language of power and oppression. *Conferred dominance*: receiving privileges you did not earn. I speak with some degree of confidence when I say that term irritates many of us in The Land of Only White. Conferred? I don't feel like royalty. I've worked for what I have. Dominance? Over what? Over whom? I sure don't feel I lord over much. And then there's that word, *privilege*.

If anything turns whites away from examining race in this country, it is this single word. *Privilege* makes us feel accused, or guilty, or angry, or resentful, or all of the above. It implies we haven't worked hard, and for most of us, that's just not accurate. I looked for a word that would be more palatable, but found nothing. White America, we're stuck with the word "privilege."

We're right back in the cave. We don't see the advantages

our skin color has bestowed upon us. We don't have to. White people say, "I don't even think about being white." And I believe them. I don't either. But therein lies the advantage. As a member of the majority in America, we can choose to think about race, or we can choose to ignore it. It is a privilege of the majority. Race does not impact our lives on a daily basis.

When it comes to race, we can choose ignorance.

Try this. Write down the first four words you would use to describe yourself. Don't analyze, just write the first four that come to mind. I share my own:

Mother

Teacher

Wife

Female

I have watched many whites formulate their list; I can't think of a time anyone wrote *white*. On the other hand, African Americans often refer to their race as one of the primary descriptors. As a minority in America, race defines them.

Once a black educator asked me one simple question that has stayed with me. "I want you to ask yourself, how much of each day do you spend thinking about race? Give it a percent."

Before teaching African American Literature, I might have said never or only occasionally. Now I upped it significantly. "Maybe 20 percent," I answered.

She nodded. "Ask someone black and most will answer something in the range of 90-100 percent. Because you're a member of the majority you have the choice, to think or not to think. You choose. I can't. I'm always thinking. Race is always an issue."

Plato said that to be enlightened one must examine, question, think. Thinking breaks the chains of blindness, but thinking about race remains a choice for white America. Blindness is comfortable.

Activist and educator Jane Elliot says we see more than we acknowledge. While we say race doesn't matter, she proves us liars. To a white audience, she often poses a simple request: "Please stand if you would be happy being treated as our black citizens are in this society." When no one stands, she repeats her directions. Still no one moves. Her response? "You know what's happening. You know you don't want it for you. I want to know why you are so willing to accept it or allow it to happen to others."[32]

White privilege is entrenched in society's structure to such a degree that we don't notice the advantage. One such policy is legacy admissions. In many of our most prestigious colleges and universities, a student is given preferential treatment in the admissions process if a parent or grandparent was an alumnus. I was unaware of this policy. What I did know was the furor over Affirmative Action, the policy designed to increase the representation of women and minorities in education and employment where they have been historically underrepresented. The controversy surrounding Affirmative Action has produced heated debates in my family and with my peers; many denounce it as reverse racism against whites.

Legacy never made it to the debate. It went under the radar, although it has clearly favored whites for generations. Harvard, which uses legacy in its admissions policy to this day, was founded in 1636. At its beginning, only white males were allowed admittance. At that time it was against the law to teach African Americans to read. Today, if you're applying to Harvard, regardless of race or gender, it means you have worked hard, but if you are white, the legacy policy may open the door of opportunity a bit wider. Generational white privilege.

And graduating from college opens other doors leading to higher rates of employment and higher paying jobs that provide more benefits. Of course, with a diploma or not, you still have to be hired. A 2008 Princeton University study on discrimination in the work place revealed that whites were more than twice as likely to be called back for job interviews than equally qualified black applicants. In fact, white applicants who admitted to felony convictions were still far more likely to be called back than black applicants with clean records. The study concluded, "Being black in America today is just about the same as having a felony conviction in terms of one's chances of finding a job."[33]

Education, employment…let's talk money. Most of us would rather have more of it. Most can admit money has its advantages. Having white parents may not feel like a privilege, but being born into wealth? Well, that's a different story. Wealth doesn't guarantee an easy ride, but it sure can help. In America, race and economics are entwined. The median net worth of whites remains nearly ten times that of black people. The disparity between white and black Americans is widening, not decreasing.[34]

The insidious dividers of race and economics have been well documented. In his compelling books *Savage Inequalities*

(1992), *Amazing Grace: The Lives of Children and the Conscience of a Nation* (1995), and *The Shame of the Nation: The Restoration of Apartheid Schooling in America* (2005), Jonathan Kozol exposes the huge disparities between public schools in affluent and poverty-stricken communities. The quality of education favors the wealthy and handicaps the poor. While providing a comprehensive view of this complex problem, Kozel humanizes his story with personal encounters. In his words, you hear the voices of children across our nation.

I do not have to travel the country to see the disparity. A span of only a few feet of hallway separating the classrooms of Honors English and African American Literature provides a microscopic view of race and economics in our society. I hear the voices of students, too.

"I can't decide which one to write about, our beach house in Australia or our condo in the mountains." I had assigned an essay in Honors English. The personal narrative was to explore the place they felt most at home. I was meeting with each student for a private writing conference. The white girl before me struggled between beach and snow. It was a real dilemma for her. Both places, thousands of miles across the globe from one another, afforded her great comfort. Both were "home" for her. Because of her family's wealth, the world was literally within her reach. And she was not unique. Another white student told me he would write of a particular street in France, another of his family's trip to the Galapagos Islands.

In the midst of these writing conferences, Marcus knocked on my office door holding a dark suit on one hanger, a freshly pressed shirt and tie on another. He asked if he could keep them in my office because his locker was too small. I complimented him on the good-looking suit, asking him what it was for. "Prom," he said simply. I hung the clothes in a safe place. Later that day, he reappeared with a fellow African American classmate. He asked for the clothes, and the two disappeared. Fifteen minutes later he was back with a smile on his face. "It fits," he said with satisfaction. I looked confused, and he continued. "My friend is borrowing the suit for prom. He doesn't have one. This is my only one, but it fits him perfectly." He was relieved, and I was left to contemplate the difference between a family that could afford a trip to the Galapagos Islands and one that could not travel to the mall to buy a jacket and a pair of pants for a school dance.

Of course these are generalities. There are privileged and wealthy black students; there are poor and homeless white students. But in our country the economic gap between whites and blacks is at its highest level in twenty-five years.[35] The pattern persists; the educational and economic gap between my two classrooms is much greater than a span of hallway.

Allow me to speak in generalities for a moment. Many of my white students are wealthy. They drive new cars to school, fly to Europe with family or on school-sponsored trips. They participate in clubs, sports, and student government, accumulating a long list of activities for college applications. They have no room for part-time jobs, but put in plenty of volunteer hours assuring acceptance into the National Honor Society. They enroll in expensive SAT prep courses, hire tutors, and see private therapists when the anxiety mounts. They own costly instruments and go to music camps. They are stretched thin with expectations and seek refuge in relaxing vacations. They challenge themselves with whitewater rafting trips, snow boarding in the mountains, and Outward Bound Survival programs. They are economically privileged, and they work hard, very hard.

Many of the black students in African American Literature ride the bus to school or catch rides with family or friends. They have not been on a plane. They are required to be childcare providers for younger siblings instead of participating in school programs or sports. They work jobs to help support their families or themselves. They work instead of volunteering or taking SAT prep courses. Music is a refuge found in headphones that filter out the harsh realities of their lives and fill their heads with songs. They do not look for ways to challenge themselves in the wilderness; challenges of survival find them. Several of my students over the years have been homeless; some have lived in shelters or cars. They are not economically privileged, and they work hard, very hard.

The expectation that I would work hard in school, that I would achieve and go to college, was an unspoken given of my youth. That there was enough money for me to choose a public university or a private college was also understood. I took this for granted, grateful without seeing it as a gift. My own daughters have all graduated from college. All attend graduate schools. The same expectation of hard work was true of their upbringing. I may not have had the wealth of my parents, but most schools were open to them. I hope they saw it as a gift, but perhaps they couldn't help but take it for granted. They, as well as I, participate in conferred dominance, receiving privileges we do not earn but are bestowed upon us by birth.

And we work hard.

None of us choose our parents, but the racial and economic environment we are born into can help or hinder our futures. I don't say determine. Of course there are exceptions, but there are also persistent patterns. So busy living our lives, we don't see our part in the design.

Plato writes of the cave dwellers that they have resided there "since they were children."[36] You know where my childhood was spent? In country clubs. Here my education in white superiority advanced to a graduate level. No black people were in this student body. Actually, that's not true. There were black people: cooks, waiters, the grounds keepers, gardeners, and the woman who handed me a towel in the bathroom. They were there serving us. Certainly this was a silent curriculum on race.

Prisons and country clubs: both are designed to segregate. Prisons keep inmates from getting out. Country clubs restrict who can get in. Prisons require you to strip down and accept that you are society's lowest element. Country clubs require you to dress up and confirm you are society's elite. Both indoctrinate the inmate or member on their worth—or lack of it.

Obviously, the country clubs of my childhood didn't imprison me. Swimming pools, tennis courts, golf courses, expensive food, and drink are hardly the life of a prisoner. But while there weren't bars or barbed wire, the country club did have barriers that separated me from others, and I'm not talking fences around the fairways. I'm talking money. Wealth was a prerequisite of the club. Because race is so entwined with economics in our country, I was in a segregated population without even knowing it: the wealthy white in The Land of Only White.

I was born into wealth; my parents were not. A butcher and a coal miner's daughter, my father and mother were children of working class families. They weathered the Depression, and without a college degree, my father achieved financial success. I don't think they took their wealth for granted. I don't even think they fully trusted it was real or that it would last. But for me, wealth was the norm. When you are born into wealth, it's easy to take it for granted and harder to see it as a privilege. It's even harder not to believe you are somehow better.

My parents told me I was not. They told me we were just like everyone else. They told me we were lucky, and my dad worked very hard. But just as my daughter came home with the message that being white was better, the message that wealth made me special seeped in from some elusive source. In America, money bestows status; therefore, it's easy to link wealth with worth. It's hard to ignore socio-economic class distinctions, and money defines our class. The more money we have, the better off we are. It's easy for the message to be condensed: we are not only *better off*—we are simply *better.*

In 1926, F. Scott Fitzgerald wrote,

> Let me tell you about the very rich. They are different from you and me. They possess and enjoy early, and it does something to them, makes them soft where we are hard, and cynical where we are trustful, in a way that, unless you were born rich, it is very difficult to understand. They think, deep in their hearts, that they are better than we are because we had to discover the

> compensations and refuges of life for ourselves. Even when they enter deep into our world or wink below us, they still think that they are better than we are. They are different.[37]

As a child, I didn't know anything about feeling "soft" or "cynical." I do know that I was proud of my father in a way that made me puff out my chest. I attended public school. All my friends were from the middle or upper class, but I remember understanding I was one of the wealthiest, and I liked it.

I remember celebrating Easter at the country club. In my frilly white dress and shiny white shoes, I searched for hidden Easter eggs. We all wanted the sparkling gold ones. They held silver dollars instead of candy. Christianity at the country club. Those searching for golden eggs as children often continue to have economic privileges supporting their future paths. I did, having conferred dominance without realizing it. Even now, some fifty years later, I continue to benefit.

When a societal system works for you and places you on top, it's easy not to question why; in fact, it's easy to believe it is only because of your own merit that you are there. I used to trust in an American system of meritocracy, that we all stood on an equal playing field and individual effort determined your fate. I wanted that belief to last. I wanted it to hold true even if I tried out this new vocabulary of power and oppression. If I travel to a foreign country and speak the language, I still want to return home. But once I applied the terms of overt, covert, institutional, and internalized racism, plus conferred dominance to my life, home was forever altered. Words do have the power to change one's perception.

I am struck by a particular memory. Once a psychiatrist came into my classroom as a guest speaker. With blunt honesty, a student asked, "Why go see you? Talking doesn't change anything."

The doctor's response was equally direct: "A good therapist gives the client a language to understand their pain. Words have the power to heal." He went on to explain that whether consumed by debilitating anxiety, grief, guilt, or anger, a therapist can help the client construct a language to find a way out of their pain. Ironically, the terms I learned in the language of oppression led me into the pain, of truth. Plato understood this: If a cave dweller were freed and "forcibly dragged up the steep and rugged ascent…dragged out into the sunlight, the process would be a painful one."[38]

I now know that America's playing field is an uneven mess. I've been humbled. It isn't only my merit that allows me to soar, and Plato was right. Sunlight hurts your eyes when you've lived in a cave since childhood.

The Privilege to Dream

Financial security is a well-crafted phrase, but we get caught up in the first word and forget the essence of the second, *security*. It's easy to distinguish wealthy students by what they have: designer clothes, cars, computers, opportunities for travel, tutors, and their college tuitions paid. These are the obvious outward financial advantages, but they have more. I now believe *security* is the greatest privilege often bestowed on the rich and stripped from the poor. And it is more than the safety net that money provides. It is the security to envision a future, to believe in education's power to transform your life. It is the security that allows you to dream.

Students who excel academically believe education is the path to a successful future. They labor in the present not because they are innately smarter than others but because they are secure in education's promise: effort now will pay off later. Parents instill these beliefs because the system worked for them. Time for academics and a quiet place to study are provided. They monitor their students' academic progress carefully to preserve the dream. There are plenty of role models in the family to give concrete evidence of education's pathway to economic stability and social status. Outside the home, society's voice confirms that white and wealthy students will be successful. You can be a doctor, a lawyer; you can even walk on the moon. Confident in the educational system and their worth in society, these students are secure enough in the present to dream their futures.

But dreams require space, and space is a luxury. Many of my African American students live crowded, chaotic lives. Dreams of a future are consumed by survival in the present.

Malik, a student athlete, has a chance for a football scholarship. My joy is not mirrored in his face. Sullen and reserved, he tells me he cannot go away to college. He has young siblings he must protect. His father is absent. His mother's frustrations vacillate between explosive outbursts of anger and depression that lead her to drink. She is unavailable mentally and unexpectedly gone from home for days at a time. They live in a small apartment, and he and his younger brothers sleep in the same room. Sometimes, when his mother can't pay the rent, they move in with other family members. He succeeds in school, but it cannot be his priority. His siblings are.

Keisha dresses, feeds, and walks her siblings to school and meets them at the end of the day because her mother works three jobs to support her children. When they are sick, she cares for them. Her residence is never permanent. When there is work, there is a roof over their heads. When there is not, they are homeless. Both Malik and Keisha raise these children, and as good parents, they place their siblings' needs above their own. It leaves little time to dream of a future. It seems selfish to do so.

For Malik and Keisha, and many other students, faith in education's promise for the future has faltered. There is neither time nor quiet space to study in their homes. Parents often don't attend parent-teacher conferences, sometimes because of unpredictable working schedules but often because they felt unwelcomed in school as students themselves. They care about their child's academic success, but find it hard to invest in a system that failed them. Role models who attended college are few or non-existent. Many students tell me they will be the first to attend college in their family; some tell me they will be the first to graduate high school. Education's power and potential is an abstract concept lacking living examples in their households. And while Barack Obama may offer proof anyone can become president, most societal messages still confirm you won't get far. Security in the system is weak; society confirms they are worth less than their white counterparts, and dreams of education's promise for the future are tenuous at best.

At the beginning of the hour, I place a piece of candy on each student's desk telling them, "You can eat this if you want, but if you leave it and give it back to me at the end of the hour, tomorrow I'll give you more."

A student eyes me intently. "Is this a trick? Will you really give me more?"

"I will. I promise."

This process is repeated for many days, and I am true to my word. Some students eat, especially if it is the hour before lunch. They don't receive anymore the next day. But many hold out, and their pile of candy grows. I end the experiment when I can't finance the activity any longer. On that final day, some sit empty-handed; others begin enjoying the stash they have amassed or pocket it for later. And this concept of *later* is just what this exercise is all about.

I have mimicked the Stanford Marshmallow Experiment

(1972), a study of immediate verses delayed gratification. In the original study young children were offered a marshmallow. They could eat it right away, but if they could wait fifteen minutes, they were promised a second marshmallow. Fifteen minutes is a long time. About one third of them waited; the others could not resist.

Initially, the experiment examined impulse control. Observing these children revealed that those able to forgo eating for greater reward in the future often had a strategy to distract themselves. They sang a song to pass the time; they looked away from the marshmallow. Researchers wondered if children could be taught methods of self-control. Many of my own students employed strategies to avoid eating also. Some asked if I could keep the candy on my desk instead of placing it on theirs for the whole hour: out of sight, out of mind, avoiding temptation. If I offered an assortment, many chose candy they didn't like in order to discourage themselves from eating it, knowing they would be able to choose again the next day.

But what the Stanford experiment showed years later held the most significance. These children were followed through their educational careers. When they graduated from high school, their SAT scores correlated with their earlier decision to eat now or wait for more. Those who could resist the marshmallow as children had higher SAT scores as teenagers.[39] This is what educators are always preaching: sacrifice pleasures of the moment (in this case, a plump marshmallow), for the greater rewards education will bring in the future (far more than a second white puff). Turn off the television, video games, music videos, and study for the greater gains in the future. Curtail your social life now for social status later. Don't let the immediate gratifications of alcohol, drugs, or sex keep you from your long-term goals. Focus on the distant horizon.

My students are then presented the Stanford study. There are films that show children struggling to resist the marshmallow. We all laugh as one little girl pops the sugary morsel into her mouth before the researcher is even through giving her the instructions. Those that ate my candy the first day identify with her. We talk about whether they see a connection with school, about whether being able to resist the temptations of the moment will make them a better student. Almost all agree. They know the words to the sermon they have heard from teachers for years: "Work hard now, and the future will be great."

What teachers may be missing is that for some of our students it isn't just immediate pleasures we're asking them to ignore, but immediate responsibilities. Malik and Keisha don't do drugs; they do day-care. Social life has already been sacrificed in order to raise siblings, not test scores. Asking them to keep their eye on the distant prize of education is asking them to turn away from family now. What do teachers see? The surface: students who seem disinterested.

Ethan, an African American boy who should be a senior, will never graduate because he has so few credits. In class he smiles all the time, socializes constantly, and makes me mad. When I get tired of failing him on every assignment, I finally talk to him. He tells me he must care for his aunt who suffers from dementia. His parents both work until late at night, and Ethan spends everyday with a woman who no longer knows him. He is alone, and school is his only break. It is his chance to be a child and not a caregiver. He has long ago given up on the idea that education will change his future. Poet Langston Hughes wrote of "a dream deferred," and this has happened to Malik, Keisha, Ethan, and many others. Deferred long enough, a dream just dies or as Hughes questioned, "does it explode?"[40]

Death doesn't discriminate between my two classes. It walks freely between Honors English and African American Literature. I have lost too many students. Drowning, car accidents, suicides…it is something no education class ever prepared me for. And I have watched students grieve the loss of a grandparent, parent, sibling, and friend, to disease or accident. But in African American Literature, too many have seen life end abruptly because of violence. Too many African American students share the experience of seeing someone shot. They recount their stories: an acquaintance at a party that went out of control, a friend on the street, a cousin in a fight, a brother outside his home. They have lost family and friends to guns. One of my students was shot by the police. Another was killed in a random shooting at a park. *Random* loses its meaning if it happens frequently. It can start to feel like fate, and security in any future fades.

On June 30, 2009, seven students waiting for the bus after attending a summer session at Cody High School in Detroit, Michigan, were shot. Their ages were between fourteen and sixteen. I listened to the news report and heard an eighteen year-old girl who witnessed the shootings remark, "It isn't right when someone so young is shot. I've at least had my life. It isn't right." If she believes eighteen years constitutes a full life, what future did she envision for herself?

I assign an essay that asks my senior students to reflect on moments that changed their lives. Andre writes of watching his mother shot dead on Christmas day. Shortly after, his father went to prison. He has been in and out ever since. In class discussions, Andre speaks of his plans to attend college. Privately, he shares he doesn't believe he will live to be thirty, or if he does, prison might be his residence.

Marcus tells me he has lost a brother. I share that I lost a brother in a car accident when I was seven. For a moment, we share common ground. Then he continues. "My brother's not dead. He's in prison." His loss is not unique to many African American students. Andre and Marcus try to dream, but both believe their father, mother, or brother's fate will find them. The future holds little reality to them.

"Black on black crime." We, in The Land of Only White, know the phrase. It allows us to distance ourselves completely. Surely we can't be held responsible when *they* decide to kill themselves. We have no such phrase for us. White on white crime is statistically far greater than black on black, but we don't know that.[41] The color of your skin does not make you commit crimes, but unemployment, poverty, and poor education do. Add in a societal message that you are less and always will be, and ask yourself what you might do to survive? How frustrated and angry might you become? But we don't ask ourselves these questions. Nathan McCall offered me two perspectives on so-called black on black crime that have stayed with me, writing, "When your life in your own mind has no value, it becomes frighteningly easy to try to take another's life," and, "Of the many things a black man can die from, the first may be rage—his own or someone else's."[42] I wonder if placed under the same conditions, what might I do? Rage seems very likely. It doesn't justify or excuse crime, but it makes me think instead of dismissing black on black violence as something unique to a population I hope to never see.

Educators look at test scores to predict academic success. I think we should have a dream-score. I'm serious. We need a dream-o-meter. Your ability to dream will predict which side of the achievement gap claims you: success or failure. Perhaps that is the greatest privilege many in White America take for granted: the security to dream a future and the means to bring the dream into reality. We don't realize that for many Americans its promise remains a deceptive illusion, a taunting and unattainable nightmare.

SIGHT

REVISION

MALCOLM X WROTE, "education is the passport to the future,"[43] and that's where I want my students' focus to be, dreaming and determining their futures. But before educators stand in front of students, I want them to do the opposite. I want them to confront their past.

English teachers assign a lot of writing: *Which character in the novel do you identify with? What was the protagonist's greatest flaw? What questions would you pose to the author?* Without pause, students scribble away, hurrying to complete the task. As they are up out of their seats and ready to hand in the assignment, I often ask them to spend a little more time, look over it, revise it. The majority say, "Why? I'm done."

That simple response resonates with many adults when it comes to their deep-seated beliefs. "I know what I believe. Why look again? I'm done."

You know *what* you believe, but do you know *why*? Are they really your own beliefs or just ones you accepted? In our pasts, many wrote upon us: first parents, then those just outside the family, and then society at large scripted its influence. Many authors pen their truths into us without our personal evaluation because we trust the source, not necessarily the idea. Sometimes a single event, for better or worse, writes a paragraph into our lives that, unawares, we generalize into a fact we then base chapters of living upon.

Extrapolating from Socrates', "The unexamined life is not worth living," I now believe we must examine most critically what we have not written ourselves. America values action not self-examination. But when it comes to race, we need reflection before reaction; in fact, considering all the committees I joined to close the achievement gap, we needed thought even before talk. Thought was what was missing. Most teachers aren't intentionally racist, but if we aren't willing to examine the prejudices that walk right in the door within us, those prejudices will damage students.

Reflection must lead to revision, the most important part of the writing process.

My third rule is to *Write Well.* When I ask students to look again at their work, they often confuse the complex process of revision with the simple task of correction. They fix misspelled words, clean up incomplete sentences, and add transitions between paragraphs. That is not revision.

Revision means to "see again," to look from a fresh and critical perspective in order to rewrite.[44] Ultimately, it means finding your own voice and writing your own truth.

Finding your "voice" is crucial. We don't want writers who merely imitate another's work or write what they believe the teacher wants to read. It is the same for the pages of our own life. Until we look back into our own pasts, asking where our convictions have come from and whether or not we actually agree with them, they are not our own. We are merely mimicking the words of others. When you read your past, reflecting on where and why your beliefs took hold, you become the authentic author of your own life in the present. Of course, that might mean beliefs need revision. We must separate ourselves for a moment, and read our long-trusted assumptions as editors with critical eyes. In fact, when it comes to looking at our beliefs, it might mean looking through someone else's eyes for a change. We need Plato's *other* to challenge what we have accepted as our reality.

This is no small feat. As educator Lisa Delpit writes, "To put our beliefs on hold is to cease to exist as ourselves for a moment—and that is not easy."[45] Our old self may be erased in the revision, but our potential new self is then genuinely our own. Beliefs can be rewritten. They are not set in stone. We have that power, but only if we find the courage to admit when we are wrong.

Malcolm wrote about nurturing a "flexibility" of mind. Age often seems to bring not only a rigidity of the body but also the brain. He knew we must be vigilant against a rigor mortis of the intellect, writing, "Despite my firm convictions, I have been always a man who tries to face facts, and to accept the reality of life as new experience and new knowledge unfolds it. I have always kept an open mind, which is necessary to the flexibility that must go hand in hand with every form of intelligent search for truth."[46]

He practiced what he preached. In his early years, Malcolm believed all whites were devils—literally. "History proves that the white man is a devil."[47] His own personal history served to support his claim. His father, Earl Little, was a Baptist minister who preached a message of pride and dignity for the black race in the Jim Crow Era. White people silenced him for it, beating him and leaving his body on train tracks to be severed in half. Many of Malcolm's relatives died violently by white hands.

For a time Malcolm believed he had found his voice as a minister in the Nation of Islam, preaching a gospel of black superiority and white hate. But he continued to question, to search for truth, and found that instead of his own voice he was nothing but a mouthpiece for Elijah Muhammad, the Nation's corrupt and hypocritical leader. He broke from the Nation and spoke for himself, now hating the *system* of racism in America, not the individual white man. He preached a doctrine of dignity for all human beings. Bullets silenced it, but Malcolm X had found his voice.

Once you find it, you must speak.

Silence Sustains Systems

You want to get students' attention? Pull out a five-dollar bill, and tell them that one of them can have it. Every school year begins with the money game. Choosing a random group of about seven students, I ask them to sit in a circle. (Random is a lie because just by the way they entered the room, I've had a chance to note some of the loudest personalities and those more reserved. Both are included in my mix.) They move chairs; the others watch closely.

Placing the money in the center, some student always makes a swipe for it. Keeping my hand on it, I present the rules: students will have three minutes to decide which of the seven students in the circle will get the cash. They may not take a vote or play random games of chance to determine the sole winner. This is no "paper-scissor-rock" activity. They must discuss and arrive at a unanimous decision. All must voice their agreement. The student awarded the money may not share it with anyone. It is theirs and theirs alone. If they can't decide in the allotted time, I get my money back.

Skeptical, they want to know if this is for real? What teacher gives away five bucks on the first day? But the discussion begins. A couple vocal students control the conversation. Others tentatively mumble a thought. There is always at least one who remains silent. Sometimes they succeed in coming to consensus, and I lose my money. Most times they fail, and I collect my cash.

I ask the whole class what was the point of this activity. Confidently, someone always answers, "To see if we could work together."

They are intrigued when I answer with the same confidence, "Nope."

I ask, "Regardless of the outcome, did everyone in the group have a voice in the decision making process? Did we actually hear from everyone?" Students replay the scene in their minds. They call out ones who dominated the conversation and those who never spoke. Both are equally accused. I ask them to think about how this exercise mirrors their experience in previous classrooms.

Teachers can count on the consistent talkers. It becomes easy for both teacher and students to rely on them. Sometimes the sheer volume or frequency of certain voices drowns out others; the rest give up, stop raising their hand to speak and are relegated to silence. Some never venture in. They are used to being mute.

I tell them, "In this class it will be different. We need to hear from everyone. Class participation grades will not only be determined by what you contribute but also how you encourage others to speak and how well you listen." Now some are angry.

"It's their own fault if they don't talk."

I ask them to think if silence really means someone had nothing to say. Finally, I state, "Here, in this class, everyone's voice is needed." And then I tell them about Devon.

Devon has long since graduated. He is a man, and I wonder where he is today. In high school everyone knew him.

Most thought he was cool; nearly all were afraid of him. I will never forget him. His steely green-gray eyes looked right through you. With a sinewy build, everything about him was fluid—his walk and his talk. His tough façade and quick intelligence were hard to ignore. I wondered why his peers both adored and feared him, but I was sure he was worthy of both.

I put Devon in the money game circle. He listened patiently to my rules, and when the discussion began, he grabbed the money, proclaiming clearly, "It's mine." Everyone consented, and then it was silent. I lost my five dollars in five seconds.

Devon is a memorable character, but also a metaphor for all that silences a voice. Some don't speak from intimidation or because they don't believe any will listen; some only mimic what they believe others want to hear; some need time to think before standing up to a force like Devon. And some never find their voice at all.

For years, I thought I had a voice. I was wrong.

Once a women's book club in a local church contacted me to suggest their next read. Assuring me they were all well-educated, they wanted a challenge. *Moby Dick* came to mind first, but many of them had already accomplished it. "How about *The Autobiography of Malcolm X*?" No one had read it. They agreed, with the qualification that I would lead the discussion after they finished it.

A few weeks later we gathered in an opulent home, luxury cars lining the driveway. I remember one in particular, a slick white sports car. Wine was poured, and I asked for these white and well-educated women their initial reaction to the book. The first comment was said with certainty:

"I don't understand why he has to be so angry. It just isn't necessary."

While the comment surprised me, it shouldn't have. Most of the women and I shared the same upbringing. We had been taught as little girls that anger was frowned upon, a sign of poor upbringing, especially if you were a woman.

Being "polite" was the expectation that ruled my childhood. I was indoctrinated in the dogma of Politeness with a capital P. There were many tenets, a complex doctrine to be learned. My mother was the primary teacher, but I also went to Charm School (there really was such a thing, and they still exist). I actually attended two sessions. There we learned the etiquette and expectations of a refined lady. We learned to be *charming*, and above all, polite. Groomed in the social graces, we were trained to sit properly, legs crossed at the ankles, never the knees, feet discreetly pulled back by the side of your chair. We mastered the art of formal table settings, able to distinguish a salad, dinner, and dessert fork and their appropriate placement. We practiced sipping soup—the spoon drawing away from you, never toward—and drinking tea from fine china cups without making a sound, your pinkie curling toward the cup, never forming an ill-mannered point. Your mouth was closed when you chewed your food; your mouth was expected to remain closed most of the time.

My favorite sessions included makeup and manicures, subtle shades for lips and nails: blushing rose, delicate pink, soft peach. All of it was quite lovely, and I asked to go to a second session where we would learn how to walk appropriately and participate in a fashion show. It was fun, a school for cultured young women.

It was only much later that I thought about the books.

Books weren't read in Charm School. Instead, they were placed on your head to teach you to move gracefully. You moved tentatively so as not to disturb the balance. I guess we didn't need to read. Charm School promoted the image, not the intellect. We cultivated charm: conversations were reserved for pleasantries, not heated debates. Pretty pink lips were most appropriate when closed in a silent smile. We were taught to be quiet, trained not to have a voice.

My mother continued Charm School's lessons in our home. She was the professor of politeness, and I, the student always in need of remediation.

AN ANGRY DONNA REED

"BEHIND EVERY GREAT MAN is a great woman." My mother's favorite proverb. She, like many of the women in her generation and circumstance, located herself accordingly "behind" her husband. Married in 1933, she was taught to support and serve her spouse in the home. The husband walked out the door to provide for the family; wives stayed behind raising children and creating a refuge for the working man. My mom recited the proverb so often I had it memorized at an early age. I liked it, believing it honored my parents' relationship. My dad certainly filled the spotlight. It seemed the proverb praised him while also honoring my mom backstage in the darkness. Now, I'm not so sure: I think instead of celebrating her, it may have served to silence her and many of the women of her time. Perhaps she repeated it so often because she was trying to convince herself of its validity.

She constructed her life around it. Her total identity came from my father. She was *Mrs. Jim Bronson* and proud of the title. She had married a great man: loyal husband, loving father, successful provider. Climbing the corporate ladder, his voice resonated with power and prestige. People applauded. She worked at home without recognition.

My mother's role model was Donna Reed, star of *The Donna Reed Show*, (1958-1966) a television sitcom that she watched faithfully. Donna made the proverb shine. She was the all-American housewife who stayed behind cooking, cleaning, and raising children. When her husband returned home, she served him with a smile. He was the great man, a doctor. She was the great woman behind him: smart, intuitive, serving her family and solving its problems. Eternally home and happy, Donna Reed was Charm School's protégé, never questioning her role. Polite women accepted society's expectations. They had no need of questions that might lead to discontent.

My mother adopted Donna's style, always in a dress with an appropriate string of pearls demurely draped around her neck. She cooked three meals a day, telling me, "Dad brings home the bacon, and I cook it." And she cleaned house with fervor. It could never be clean enough.

But she just couldn't seem to stay happy. She told me to trust the tenets of her life and never question them, but she was a housewife for over sixty years and I think, while she tried to deny them, questions haunted her. They made her mad, mostly at herself for not being content with the dictates of her generation, for being a charm school failure.

I wish my mother could have read Malcolm X. He would have helped her see that in allowing society's expectations to define her, she had placed herself in prison. In reality, she had choices. She could have gone to college and worked outside the home. There were opportunities, but she did not allow herself to consider them and, in the process, lost her confidence. In elevating my father so high, she lost her own footing. The higher he went, the lower her self-esteem seemed to fall. She didn't just place herself behind my father; she placed herself below him.

Her frustration may have erupted because she wanted to be recognized in her own right. I think she wanted a small piece of the stage but felt like a failure for not being silent and content behind the curtain. When my father was gone from home, she raged but was heard only by the small audience of me. She raged when I walked across the living room carpet disturbing the perfect pattern she had worked so hard to create with the vacuum cleaner; when she couldn't iron my father's pants to perfection or remove a stain from his shirt; when my hair was messy, and I didn't care. Raged at the boredom of days with no place to go and at me when I walked out the door.

Malcolm X would have helped her claim her anger and identify its actual origins. He would have encouraged her to find the language of her rage, the words that could have freed her to construct her own life. He could have helped her find her voice, but she would not have read Malcolm X because he was a black and angry man. Both adjectives forbade her entrance.

Those same adjectives took life in the form of my students when I began teaching African American Literature. Of course, I had met angry white students, but for the most part, theirs was individual rage over individual circumstances. In African American students I sensed a shared, collective anger. I can remember white students saying to me, "Why are black students always so angry?" I was too polite to speak it, but I shared this question. What was their problem? Just like the woman in the church book club, I silently judged their anger to be unnecessary.

Now, standing in front of a classroom of African American

students, I felt the presence of an anger I didn't understand. It was not directed at me; its source was racism at an almost visceral level I could have never understood. Writing provided a language for them to speak their experience. Each had a story, and writing gave them a voice they often felt had gone unheard. I read every word they wrote. Unexpectedly, they helped me understand my mother.

As a white and wealthy woman, she never suffered the injustices of racism in this country. She never feared for her life, was never denied the right to vote, or forbidden to use a drinking fountain because of the color of her skin. Well, except once: she told me of traveling in the South in the 1940s with my older sister and brother. They had stopped for gas and a bathroom break. Noticing two drinking fountains, one marked *Whites* and the other, *Colored*, she made the assumption that the one labeled *Colored* would light up like a rainbow and quickly placed my siblings in this line. A white attendant at the gas station immediately appeared at her side. "You trying to make trouble?" he asked sternly.

Her naive response, "No, I just wanted the kids to see the pretty water."

My mother led what most would consider a privileged life, but she also felt powerless and silenced by the expectations of her era. Today African American students tell me of life in a society that continually reminds them that they are less. They feel invisible and without a voice, disenfranchised and diminished, just as I believe my mother had. Before reading the words of these students and of Malcolm X, before this education I began to receive, I just saw my mother as an angry Donna Reed. Now, I see her as a part of a system much greater than herself.

One of the greatest lessons Malcolm X taught was that any system of oppression tries to sustain itself. Racism and sexism both lived in the past, but they continue to breathe in our present. They do not go down easily.

I didn't realize the sexism of my mother's time still touched me. Instilled in me was the belief that anger was unnecessary and impolite. Good little white girls avoided anger: their own and other people's. But I couldn't avoid my students. They taught me not to turn away from anger.

Robert was a ticking time bomb, and it only took twenty minutes for him to explode. He came in the middle of the school year, in the middle of a class period. I had been told only to expect a new student. He came in, sitting down near my student teacher. Like the calm before the storm, there was an eerie silence about him, full of electricity. You could almost hear the sirens going off to take cover. I ignored the warning, continuing to teach and was in mid sentence about something literary when he jumped up, tipping over his desk. He towered over my student teacher.

"What the fuck you looking at, bitch?" he screamed directly in her face. My student teacher cowered, and I moved to the door asking Robert to join me in the hall. He did, but the cyclone had touched ground. Every empty desk in his path was upended as he exited.

In the hall, he said flatly, "You may not have noticed, but I have anger management problems." The irony of his words made me smile, but the next line was like a slap. "So, you're going to throw me out just like everyone else."

I never did throw Robert out, but the school ultimately

did. In the next few weeks, he had several explosions in other classes. Some got physical. A major fight in the hall was the last offence. Administrators said they could not accommodate someone with his issues; he didn't belong in a public school. They expelled him for good.

Perhaps the school was right. His rage jeopardized the safety of others; he needed more psychological support than we could provide. But Robert was also right. Just as he had predicted, he was thrown out. I learned he had been shuffled between family members since he was baby and then into foster care. There was always a new home that never lasted. No one wanted this child. He had been tossed away by many. Anger was his defense against despair.

My introduction to Jay came in the form of a statement from his counselor. "If we can keep him in school, he could really go far. He's got an anger problem, but he's very bright." He wasn't tall, but all muscle. When he turned the evil eye on you and puffed himself up, the message was that he could mess you up. I don't think he lied. I don't know why I never feared him. Maybe it's because in those eyes I could still see the little boy who seemed so hurt.

I told him privately that his look didn't work on me. He smiled. From then on the Jay in class remained the same menacing figure, but out of the spotlight, he was a gentleman with me. No matter how many times I asked him what made him so mad, he wouldn't tell me. Finally, he shared what raged in him with the whole class.

We were reading *Native Son*. I was lecturing about symbolism, how Richard Wright used the white snow to represent the protagonist's feelings of being frozen out by the white world. A few students looked interested; most thought I was making it up. Jay didn't care about snow in or out of a novel.

Attempting to engage students personally, I asked them to bring in their own symbols to present to the class. In fact, I wanted three from each of them, objects that represented their past, present, and future. Now, at least I had their attention.

We talked about the definition of a symbol, something concrete that represents something abstract. Richard Wright's snow might not seem concrete, but it was something you could touch. Snow represented the cold, white world, something more immense that what you could hold in your hand. When I assigned them to bring in three symbols of their own, they asked me for examples. Pausing for a moment, I pointed to a ring on my finger that holds each of my daughters' birthstones. "This ring symbolizes my family," I said. "They are always with me like this ring is always on my finger. They are valuable to me. I would use this ring to represent my present because my children are my greatest treasures." I thought for a moment. "To represent my future, I might bring in a clock because I feel like I'm running out of time."

They might not have been listening about Richard Wright's use of symbols, but they were attentive now. Questions erupted, "Can I bring in a basketball?"

"What does it symbolize?"

"Basketball."

"Then no," I answered, "because it *is* a basketball. It doesn't symbolically represent a basketball. It might represent the love you have for your team, or hard work, or a coach who made a difference in your life."

Students' understanding deepened beyond a rote definition. I gave them the rest of the hour to think, talk, and question each other about the objects they would bring in the next day. I reminded them they didn't have to reveal anything too personal, just something that captured an aspect of their past, present, and future. And I stressed their grade would depend on having three, separate, objects.

If I had held to my requirements, I would have missed the poignant power of Jay's presentation the next day. When he strode to the front of the classroom with only a single balloon in his hand, I knew better than to cross him in public, but privately I planned to ask him why someone as bright as him didn't fulfill the assignment of three.

His opening statement grabbed all of our attention. "Teacher wants to know what makes me mad. I'm finally going to tell her. When I think of my childhood," Jay's powerful voice was softer than I had ever heard. We struggled to hear him, "I think of a balloon. For a very short time, before my dad went to prison, things were good. It was fun. I had balloons at my birthday parties; I was happy."

He stopped and blew into the balloon a little. "When he went to prison, everything changed." He blew some more, his voice getting louder. "Everything changed just like this balloon is changing. But the balloon doesn't represent my childhood anymore. That's over. Now the balloon represents all the anger I feel inside." He blew in a lot more air, the balloon dangerously close to breaking. "This is how I feel now. Like I'm about to explode—I might." We all believed him.

He paused, looking at it as if it was a mirror. "For my future," he let out a little of the air, "I need to find a way to calm down." He let out more, and then let it go. The balloon zipped out of his hand and flew. "I need to find a way to let go of my anger so I can go some place in life." Walking back to his seat the class seemed to be holding their breath; some nodded to Jay as he walked by. Then they all turned their eyes on me. All I could think to say was, "Jay gets an A." They agreed.

After that, Jay and I forged a friendship. He worked in class and stayed late to talk. Then one day he came into class looking like that bursting balloon, stretched taunt and thin. When a student bumped into him, rage was his release. As I pulled him into the hall, he whispered, "My cousin got shot. He's dead."

From then on Jay was often absent or like a ghost when he appeared. I didn't see the anger anymore. I didn't see anything at all. He was like the deflated balloon, but I don't know where he went. He stopped coming to school. I don't know what happened to him. It was then that I learned an angry student is nothing to be afraid of. It means they are still alive.

If I had held to my requirements, I would have missed the poignant power of Katrina's presentation the next day. She was a big, black girl who sat sullenly at the back of the room. Sullen, but not silent. Angry outbursts directed at other students were a near daily occurrence. I never saw what provoked her, but her peers knew to keep their distance. She sent me the same message. She did just enough work to pass with a disinterested D. At sixteen, she seemed more like an exhausted and bitter old woman. She would, however, write. In the pages of her journal I began to learn about her life. Her father had disappeared when she was thirteen, her mother's time was consumed providing for five younger siblings and finding work. Katrina lived in a crowded house, alone.

I have forgotten some of the words she wrote, but I will never forget her symbol. "This is my object," she stated while pulling an old wool scarf out of a paper bag. I don't know why, but I immediately interrupted. "You need three." Those rigid requirements just didn't want to go down without a fight.

"This is three," she snapped. I could see us both positioning for a collision. I told her to go on. She put the scarf carefully around her neck, smoothing it out so it draped over her shoulders. It looked old but still beautiful. "When I was little my mom had a warm hold on me, just like this scarf. She made me feel safe. She made me do things right in school, everywhere. I knew she was there, holding me tight. We had a good family; it was perfect. My mom, my dad…I had it all. That was my past."

She loosened the scarf a little. "When I got in middle school, my mom was still there with me, but she cut me a little slack. She wasn't as strict; she was a mom and a friend. I'd talk to her about everything, even boys." She let the scarf fall off one shoulder. "But then things started to change. My dad…" She paused, and now she didn't look at us. "I lost him, but it felt like I lost my mom too. I didn't feel her around as much. She's gone a lot working, and when she is home, she just spends time with my baby brothers. I don't think she sees me at all except to tell me to do things." The scarf fell to the floor. "That's my present."

Then Katrina picked it up and put it carefully around her shoulders. "Now in my future, I'm learning to do things on my own. I don't trust that anyone will ever really be there. I'm going to have to keep myself safe and warm." She turned in a circle so we could see the entire scarf carefully in place. She had more than fulfilled the assignment with just one object.

The scarf was soft and warm. Katrina's anger was hard and cold, but I could see the similarity. She wore her anger like armor, defending her against anyone who could ever hurt her again.

The most frightening student I ever had was Aisha. Her mother moved her out of a crime-ridden neighborhood in Chicago after her daughter's boyfriend had been shot and killed. She didn't want to lose her daughter to the violence, but looking at her, I was afraid she already had. Her face showed nothing. No expression at all. She sat in the back of the class sometimes doing work, sometimes not. She rarely spoke to students or to me. I tried every trick I'd learned in thirty years to crack through her deafening quiet. When I met with her mother she told me she had started to slip into silence two years before when she and her husband had divorced. When the boyfriend had been shot, she knew she needed to move, to start again, but Aisha's detachment was complete. I had Aisha as a freshman and again as a senior in African American Literature. Her demeanor never changed. She walked across the stage at graduation as if she had resigned herself to a future that held only the nothingness of her current existence. She was passive in her acceptance of whatever befell her. Anger would have meant she was fighting for a new life. She wasn't.

I had been taught anger was impolite and improper, showing only a weakness in upbringing. Now in my students, far from a weakness, I saw it as strength, a survival mechanism. If you're angry, you're still here. People can hear you. You haven't succumbed to the silence of despair.

Good little white girls don't get angry. It was time to grow up. For the first time in my life, I placed value in anger.

Malcolm X raged against a society that had been uncivil to him. His fiery rhetoric was a survival tactic against a nation that denigrated his entire race. He didn't want be a second-class citizen, a *boy*. He wanted to live fully as a man deserving rights and respect. Through my students' eyes, I began to see a school that was often uncivil and rude to many African American students. They saw who was held in high regard; they knew they were not. They saw who filled the honors classes; they were not there. Many stopped trying and proved the achievement gap to be true. They participated in their own underachievement because they no longer believed school was for them.

Their anger rarely targeted me; more often it was directed inward or at each other. I wondered why students weren't raging against a school system that often betrayed them. Their complacency was a form of death.

So was mine. I felt a new found anger, at myself and my fellow educators. Why weren't we raging for our students' survival? Surely, if we really believed that all students could learn, we could and would close this achievement gap. Our complacency revealed our hand in sustaining it.

As a white woman I had equated compliant with polite: stay silent, keep smiling, be pleasant. Don't question and don't make waves. It seemed to have served me well. I just hadn't realized that to remain faithful to this principle of politeness requires you to become blind to injustice.

Once you see an injustice you never knew was there, anger

begins to whisper in your ear, begging you to find a voice. And it's anger not only at the injustice you now see but in the feeling that you've been deceived by the tenets you trusted. My newfound voice got me evicted from The Land of Only White and Polite Women. Anger burned the bridge to my return.

I admit, sometimes I have wished to go back. And Plato knew this. As he wrote, the ascension into the sunlight would be "painful" leaving the freed man "at a loss."[48] So why go? Enlightenment at the price of eviction from the land we have known doesn't seem like a bargain. We, in The Land of Only White, want to know what's in it for us?

I'd like to pose three reasons: money, morality, and because we like thinking we're smart.

MONEY

MONEY MOTIVATES MOST OF US in The Land of Only White. We spend a lot of time examining what we have and dreaming of more. You can never have too much. What we don't see is that racism is robbing us blind. It costs us all.

In 2015, The Kellogg Foundation published *The Business Case for Racial Equity*. Its findings were clear:

> Moving toward racial equity can generate significant economic returns as well. When people face barriers to achieving their full potential, the loss of talent, creativity, energy, and productivity is a burden not only for those disadvantaged, but for communities, businesses, governments, and the economy as a whole. Initial research on the magnitude of this burden in the United States, as highlighted in this brief, reveals impacts in the trillions of dollars in lost earnings, avoidable public expenditures, and lost economic output.[49]

Inequities in health care, education, employment opportunities, and incarceration rates appear as separate entities but in actuality are entwined. I think of my student Vanessa, who sat through class with her head in her hands, eyes closed. Her demeanor defined her as one of the unmotivated, underachieving students who give validity to the achievement gap and sustains stereotypes. What you couldn't see was the simple fact that her tooth hurt, badly. She needed a root canal. She had seen a dentist, but without health insurance, there was no money for the procedure. The pain was unbearable, and the next day she was absent. She was absent a lot.

Inadequate health care can negatively affect school attendance. Poor attendance is linked to poor academic performance, which lead to poor employment possibilities and unemployment rates, which contribute to crime and incarceration. It's the birdcage metaphor all over again, its intricate wires twisting together to form a prison from which there is no escape. From a financial perspective, none of us in America, black or white, escape the effects of racism. To some degree, we are all contained and drained. And we are talking big money.

Ani Turner, the lead author of the Kellogg report, cites the work of a McKinsey and Company analysis of the achievement gap, stating, "Closing the education gap would have increased U.S. GDP by 2% to 4% in 2008, representing between $310 and $525 billion."[50] The report also notes the costly pairing of poor education and incarceration rates: "Students struggling with academic performance in elementary and high schools are at markedly elevated risk of high school dropout and incarceration."[51] Prison is expensive. We pay. In at least forty states, the amount per year to house an inmate far exceeds that used to educate a student.[52]

Incarceration over education.

I can hear my hard-working, tax-paying constituents in The Land of Only White: "The solution is simple: If *they* worked harder and stayed in school, *they* would have better jobs. If *they* didn't commit crimes, *they* wouldn't be in jail." If you look at who's in prison, it certainly supports that *they* are the ones with the problem. While African Americans make up approximately 13 percent of America's population, they account for nearly 40 percent of the prison population.[53] It seems logical to believe that incarceration rates correspond to crime rates.

However, they do not.

Civil Rights attorney and professor Michelle Alexander published her extensive research in *The New Jim Crow: Mass Incarceration in the Age of Colorblindness* (2010). She writes:

> Although crime rates in the United States have not been markedly higher than those of other Western countries, the rate of incarceration has soared in the United States while it has remained stable or declined in other countries.

In fact, America has the highest incarceration rate in the world.[54] And whom are we putting behind bars? Our minorities, in particular, African Americans. Alexander continues: "No other country in the world imprisons so many of its racial and ethnic minorities. The United States imprisons a larger percentage of its black population than South Africa did at the height of apartheid."[55]

Those facts fuel White America's belief. *If you do the crime, you do the time.* And what is the crime that puts most African Americans behind bars? Drugs. So that stereotype of the black drug dealer seems not to be fiction, but fact.

But let's be honest. While we hold the stereotype of the black drug dealer, most of us in The Land of Only White know there are drugs in our own communities, plenty of them.

And we sell to our own. Alexander reminds us, white people sell to white people, black people to black people, and college students to college students. Many studies show that whites have higher substance abuse rates than our minorities, yet they are the least likely to be made criminals. Black people are thirteen times more likely to be incarcerated for the same drug crime as white people.[56] So what is going on systemically? Alexander asserts we must see our criminal justice system for what it really is—a system of racial injustice.

I think of all the white people I have know who have been involved in the drug trade, including those in my extended family. Not one of them has gone to prison. It's interesting that I don't even consider those in my circle as drug dealers. That's just not a term we, in The Land of Only White, use for our own—even when it fits. Drug use remains a problem in both black and white communities, but in one it is much more likely to be seen as criminal. That allows us in The Land of Only White to condemn African Americans while excusing the same behavior in our own.

In addition to being unjust, as the Kellogg report concludes, the current system costs us financially. But the report remains hopeful: "All areas… can be influenced by targeted policies and programs."[57] Reform could make us richer. But to reform we first have to acknowledge a problem. We have to see, and we're right back in Plato's cave. Instead of blindly blaming individuals or targeted groups for their failures, we have to look for systemic flaws and recognize our place in that system. Doing so could put money in our pockets.

While white America values money, we also value our morality. We know we are good people.

MORALITY

OUR MORALS IN The Land of Only White are just fine. What my parents instilled in me, I honor and pass to my children: *Do unto others as you would have done to you.* We preach, teach, believe it. Our problem is not in our morals, but in our definition of *others.*

Others really means only us.

And this is what Plato was trying to tell us. Chained in the cave, we need some genuine *others* to help free us, but we don't see them. In fact, this other-blindness is a white American tradition:

> We hold these truths to be self-evident, that all men are created equal, that they are endowed by their Creator with certain Unalienable Rights, that among these are Life, Liberty and the Pursuit of Happiness.

The Declaration of Independence's proclamation that "all men are created equal" excluded women and African Americans held in slavery at its origin. Thomas Jefferson, primary author of the document, not only owned slaves, but fathered them as well and kept them in servitude. He didn't see others; he saw only his own: white males.

"Give me your tired, your poor, your huddled masses yearning to breathe free." The Statue of Liberty beckons all, but our history dispels the myth of inclusion. We abuse and discard others: the destruction and displacement of Native Americans, the enslavement of African Americans, the internment camps imprisoning Japanese Americans, a ban on Muslims.

All of them American, but not our clan. Our morals appear fine; it's our definition of family that stinks.

We interpret *family* quite literally. When we sit in church and speak of brotherhood, *brother* means "blood." We may broaden our definition to include some friends who look like us, but when it comes down to it, we circle the wagons around our own. When Jesus teaches, "What you do to the least of my brethren, you do to me," we think he's speaking about our crazy uncle that we rarely see. The bonds of love and responsibility unifying a family are reserved for the few. Within that small group we love deeply, completely. We are content in Plato's cave. We see no need for others.

For a long time, Malcolm X agreed with us. He first defined family as only his own black race, loving them and excluding all others. That understanding changed after his conversion to Islam, when he left America and traveled to Mecca. There he recounted, "I saw all races, all colors, blue-eyed blonds to black skinned Africans in true brotherhood! In unity! Living as One! Worshiping as one."[58] His vision and his love expanded to include others. For Malcolm X, family became humanity.

Malcolm X had left the darkness of Plato's cave, writing, "We need more light about each other. Light creates understanding, understanding creates love, love creates patience, and patience creates unity."[59]

Most of us will never travel to the other side of the world to have such a conversion, but we must still challenge the borders of our own morality. Our moral compass is broken. Instead of moving us forward, it keeps us contained in a circle of only us. Morality demands a brotherhood of mankind.

Perhaps we could begin with Americans. When Abraham Lincoln first took office as the sixteenth president, he found the nation gravely divided and on the brink of civil war. Over 150 years later, we are still a gravely divided nation in need of his words:

> We must not be enemies. Though passion may have strained it must not break our bonds of affection. The mystic chords of memory, stretching from every battle-field and patriot grave to every living heart and hearthstone all over this broad land, will yet swell the chorus of the Union, when again touched, as surely they will be, by the better angels of our nature.[60]

We need those angels to inhabit not only the church but the streets. Not platitudes mouthed in prayer, but actions carried out in practice. Or perhaps we should just lower our sights from the heavens into our humanness. British author E.M. Forster tells us to forget those "bonds of affection," those "mystic chords," and get real. We are not capable of loving others. He writes:

> The fact is we can only love what we know personally. And we cannot know much. In public affairs, in the rebuilding of civilization, something much less dramatic and emotional is needed, namely, tolerance.

> Tolerance is a very dull virtue. It is boring. Unlike love, it has always had bad press. It is negative. It means merely putting up with people, being able to stand things. No one has ever written an ode to tolerance or raised a statue to her. Yet this is the quality which will most be needed…This is the state of mind we are looking for. This is the only force which will enable different races and classes and interests to settle down together…[61]

Whether we cling to the ideal of love or the less lofty tolerance, both require we deal with *others.* Perhaps I need not love my brother, but I have to acknowledge him. In our insular definition of family in The Land of Only White we have some strange relatives. Every home has them: the strange aunt, the deadbeat cousin, the smelly grandpa, and those crazy relatives on the other side of the state who don't share our politics. We shake our head and roll our eyes, and worry about the holiday that will force us to sit across the table from them and share conversation. But still we sit. We don't understand them, but we don't discard them. We break bread together.

We know we are good people in The Land of Only White. We *say* everyone is welcomed at America's table. We just prefer to sit in a section reserved only for us. I think we've forgotten the purpose of morals: to question the gap between what we profess and what we practice, to attempt to close that gap.

It's the absence of questioning which makes us less smart than we think we are.

Don't Trust Your Teachers

Recently I visited a predominantly African American high school near Chicago. Entering the school's library, I was amazed by its beauty. Artists had been hired to create large, lifelike murals on each wall. Albert Einstein stared down from one, Nathanial Hawthorne and Mark Twain on another. A boat carrying George Washington sailed on choppy waters on the third. A statue of Hippocrates stood in the center of the room, and off to one side, next to a grand piano of polished wood, was a bust of Mozart.

Black students sat at tables reading; some roamed the room looking for something on the shelves. I do not know what they were learning from the books, but I know what the walls taught them. Education belongs to white people.

White people claim education. We like believing we're the intellectual elite, a bit brighter than the others. This is what we've been taught. Our schooling exposes us most to white accomplishments in every field, from science to the arts. This library confirms my intellectual lineage back to the great Greeks and Romans and the white Americans who came after. Why would I not believe white people are the smartest? I didn't doubt my teachers. I believed them. I didn't think I was getting only part of the story. White achievement *was* the story. And I liked being part of that exclusive club.

I never thought to question where were the people of color? What had they contributed to the intellectual history of civilization? And even more disturbing to me personally, for a long time I didn't ask about the women of the world and their achievements. Maybe I wasn't really in the club after all.

We, in The Land of Only White, profess a strong belief in education while betraying its highest tenet—to continually question everything. I trusted my teachers implicitly. Now my advice for students is, "Don't trust your teachers," which really means learn all you can from them—then question it all.

Plato knew this. His teacher, Socrates, knew it. They were engaged in, as Malcolm X wrote, an "intelligent search for truth."[62] Education has no final destination; it is the *pursuit* of knowledge. Questions drive that continuous quest. Scholars never rest in the comfort of the certain but live in the continual discomfort of the inquiry. If we claim to be educated, we must question not only what we don't know, but most important, what we think we do.

When it comes to the issue of race in America, we shouldn't rest in the lessons of our teachers, whether they stood in front of classrooms or tucked us into bed as children. We've got to embrace a healthy sense of distrust. We can't claim superior intelligence while ignoring the questions that should spring from our inconsistencies.

"IT MIGHT NOT BE FAIR, BUT IT'S RIGHT."

MARK TWAIN KNEW AMERICA'S INCONSISTENCIES. With his satirical prose, he exposed us in all our hypocritical glory. One small passage from his novel *The Adventures of Huckleberry Finn* particularly hits home for me. Twain describes the bloody feud between two families, The Grangerfords and the Shepherdsons. Ongoing for generations, no one remembers how it began, but the blood continues to flow. Except on Sundays:

> Next Sunday we all went to church, about three mile, everybody a-horseback. The men took their guns along, so did Buck, and kept them between their knees or stood them handy against the wall. The Sheperdsons done the same. It was pretty ornery preaching—all about brotherly love, and such-like tiresomeness: but everyone said it was a good sermon, and they all talked it over going home, and had such a powerful lot to say about faith and good works, and free grace, and preforeordestination…[63]

I don't know the Sheperdsons or the Grangerfords, but I know this scene was replayed in the church of my youth, not with guns but golf clubs. As soon as the sermon on brotherly love had concluded, they were out there on the fairways joking about the *Nigs*, and sharing real concerns about the black family, whose father was a doctor, moving into the neighborhood.

The family members I describe are good church-going, moral people. If they see a contradiction in their words on Sunday morning and the ones they use through the rest of the week, they don't acknowledge it. They certainly don't question it.

The need to question is the core of Twain's novel. He places the moral dilemma of slavery in Huck, a white boy who blindly accepts the practice until he forms a friendship with Jim, a runaway slave. Readers watch Huck struggle with society's twisted sense of justice until his own decision is clear. If society sentences Huck to hell for harboring a runaway, he accepts the terms. He has seen Jim as his equal. As Twain explains: "*Huck Finn* is a book of mine in which a sound heart and a deformed conscience come into collision, and the conscience suffers defeat."[64] Huck's sound heart emerges only because he is able to question what his society taught him to accept.

I knew an actual boy about Huck's age who had no such moral dilemma when it came to race in America. White, wealthy, and academically successful, Nathan sat in class as I lectured on the race riots that occurred across America in 1967. Known as "the long, hot summer of 1967," most major cities across the country had erupted in flames. Over one hundred people died. We were studying the Kerner Report, a commissioned study headed by Illinois Governor Otto Kerner, which examined all the underlying factors leading to such nationwide destruction. The likely culprits were all named including inequities in housing, education, unemployment, and a racially skewed judicial system. The Kerner Commission's conclusion in 1967 held a dire warning: face these issues or be a country divided by race—in effect, two separate Americas forever.

Now forty years later, students began discussing the disturbing similarities. Little had changed when it came to race relations, little resolved. Two separate Americas is reality. And again, separate certainly doesn't mean equal. In general, white people have better homes, schools, and jobs. Black people are the majority only in prisons. Nathan's hand went into the air, signaling he wanted to weigh in on the conversation. His tone was confident as he succinctly stated: "It might not be fair, but it's right."

I have thought about his comment for years, hearing still his voice and his certainty. He was telling me that he recognized inequities in America, but the system was sound. White people had more; black people had less. Not fair, but correct. How could he study the facts and still stand firm in his assertion?

Cognitive dissonance: I learned the term in college. Social psychologist Leon Festinger (1957) used this term when referring to the tension we feel when holding opposing ideas at the same time. Because we don't like discord, Festinger theorized that we attempt to resolve it in order to return to a state of internal consistency. For example, if I know smoking is dangerous to my health, I can quit. Issue resolved. But if I don't want to stop or can't, instead of facing facts, I can relax in rationalizations. I know smoking is dangerous, so I will continually plan on stopping instead of stopping, or tell myself I'm only a social smoker, or point to my one ancient relative who still smokes and feel confident that I too will beat the odds.

When it comes to racism, rationalization abounds in The Land of Only White. We tell ourselves: *Race isn't our problem. What's wrong with them? Slavery was in the past. I never owned slaves. They need to get over it. Everything is fine now if they only worked harder. Look how many are in prison! If they could only get it together and act more like us, we'd all be fine.* Of course, when you still don't want the black doctor who clearly "got it together" to move into your neighborhood, you'll have to increase the rationalizations, or as Festinger predicted, "actively avoid situations and information,"[65] that add to your dissonance. You'll have to bury yourself a bit deeper in Plato's cave.

But here was my student acknowledging America's racial inequities and still proclaiming it was right. No cognitive dissonance, only confidence. How could he be so sure? I had plenty of questions ready to fire at him. But none for myself.

That's what teachers do: question others. You know the old adage, "Physician, heal thyself." Well, "Teacher, question thyself!" African American journalist and educator Ta-Nehisi Coates writes in *Between the World and Me* of the need for "constant questioning, questioning as ritual, questioning as exploration rather than the search for certainty."[66] In The Land of Only White, we like certainty, especially the certainty that we are correct. White feels right. How far away, really, are we from my student's proclamation: "It may not be fair, but it's right"? Right can become righteous, and there's nothing more deadly to intelligent thought than righteousness. The righteous see no need to question themselves.

Perhaps I was more like William than I wanted to admit.

Now that's some real cognitive dissonance for me, but how else could I have been proud to say I taught in a *diverse* high school while never questioning why honors classes didn't reflect this diversity? How did I grow up believing we're all equal without wondering why I never saw anyone black in my neighborhood, or school, or church? And how did I think my family didn't see color when they told me I must never, ever date or marry a black man? Once you open the door, the questions just keep coming. I had lived with these inconsistences without discomfort. It seems incredulous to me now.

Plato would say I resided in the cave of my own ignorance, blind to the truth. I think I was also deaf.

An echo is a pretty cool phenomenon. Standing in a canyon or high on a mountain, yell out, and your own voice bounces right back at you. Cool, but not confusing. You know its your voice and not another's. However, in Plato's cave, the prisoners are unaware of their surroundings and unable to turn their heads. They might mistake their echo for the voice of someone new. Many of us in The Land of Only White might be equally confused.

While we assume we are getting our information and facts from multiple varied and reliable sources, all we may actually be hearing are our own intonations reverberating off the walls of our domain. Journalists refer to this as the "echo chamber effect." Without the voices of actual others "readers are only shown content that reinforces their current political or social views, without ever challenging them to think differently."[67] The Land of Only White is certainly an enclosed system. Without the voice of others to challenge assumptions, we become entrenched in our own truth, avoiding the troubling questions that might suggest we are wrong. We do not grow. We're comfortable; it's hard to imagine we're contained, imprisoned. Consider your own education. How many teachers did you have that weren't white? Whom did you learn from?

Malcolm X went to prison for burglary at the age of twenty. He entered, by his own admission as a street thug, a hustler, but left prison a highly educated man ready to take his place as a minister in the Nation of Islam. However, when he forgot the power of questioning, he found himself in another enclosed world as restricting as the bars of his cell. Malcolm believed he spoke with the strength of his own convictions, later realizing he was only preaching another man's certainties that were no longer his own. I found it hard to understand how one so intelligent could have given up his own mind. It took a friend of Malcolm X to help me understand.

I was in full Malcolm X lecture mode when a student raised his hand, saying casually, "My father knew him." I thought he was messing with me. Even though I had been alive during Malcolm's final years, he was a historical figure, not a real human being. He continued, "My father was his bodyguard. He was his friend."

I knew his father only as a retired policeman who worked in our building. A big bear of a man, his obvious strength had not diminished with age. Often in full Muslim attire, his white robes flowed throughout our school.

When Ahmed introduced me to him, I felt humbled. I had come to see myself as something of an expert on all things X, but my knowledge was always from secondary sources, intellectualized and removed. I had listened to Malcolm's speeches, but I had never stood in his presence. Brother Umar's profound understanding came from a personal friendship, an intimate bond of brotherhood. When Brother Umar shook my hand his was a hand that had held Malcolm's.

He was soft-spoken and calm; I was the opposite, overwhelming Brother Umar with my questions. Soon I was asking him to be a guest speaker in my classroom. His recollections were a portal into the past. His memories merged and melted into all my book learning. He told us, in contrast to the stern countenance of Malcolm X on the poster that hung in my room, Malcolm had loved to laugh and play practical jokes. He said on more than one occasion Malcolm X had replaced the sugar with salt, holding back laughter until Brother Umar had tasted his coffee. The words I had read in Ozzie Davis's eulogy for Malcolm X came alive: "Did you ever talk to Brother Malcolm? Did you ever touch him, or have him smile at you? …For if you did, you would know him. And if you knew him, you would know why we must honor him."[68] Brother Umar had felt his touch and seen his smile.

He told us Malcolm X didn't set out to be a leader, but the circumstances of the time and the power of his voice captivated an audience that was hungry to hear what he had to say. Brother Umar said he had been hungry too. A young teen and out of money in New York City, someone told him where he could get a free meal. The Nation of Islam was running a soup kitchen; the only price of admission was to listen to one of their young ministers speak. Physical hunger drove him there, but the young speaker's words satiated him.

Brother Umar tried to help us feel the black man's reality in the 1950s and 60s. He said, "It was a hard time. Brothers would go missing. The white police didn't care; in fact, they were often involved." Brother Umar never said he was frightened, but his stories evidenced it. It was hard to imagine this big and powerful man ever being afraid, but if he had been, there must have been something to fear.

In the midst of his meal in that soup kitchen, there was Malcolm X, charismatic and self-confident, telling black men not to be afraid. He told them not only to stand up to the white man, but to leave him altogether; to be independent—a nation of strong black men, no longer relegated to the status of slave or servant or boy. He told them they were not inferior but deserving of dignity. And yes, he told them white people were devils. Many in the audience, including Brother Umar and Malcolm X himself, had personal experiences that gave credence to that statement. Brother Umar joined the Nation of Islam, rising in the ranks to serve as Malcolm X's personal bodyguard.

Believing he was now a Muslim, a Black Muslim, Brother Umar blindly followed the tenets decreed by Elijah Muhammad, the head of the Nation. He gave up pork, didn't drink or use drugs, accepted that sex must wait for marriage, knew that white people were devils and black people the true superior race. Elijah Muhammad was seen as either a holy messenger or God himself. His followers did not question his teachings. Initially, Brother Umar said unquestioning allegiance was a small price to pay. In the Nation he had value; in American society, he had none. But the price finally became too great for Malcolm X and ultimately for Brother Umar. Rather than divine, both men came to see Elijah Muhammad as a flawed mortal who twisted the tenets of Islam for his own purposes.

Both men left the Nation.

Each time Brother Umar talked to my class, his memories of the past spoke directly to my students in the present. He told them the essential problem was that the Nation, at that time, didn't want you to question anything. He told my students to read everything they could get their hands on. He told them to question always.

The ritual of questioning gives sight to blind eyes and sound to deaf ears. But I fear that in the enclosed system of The Land of Only White, we are not only blind and deaf—we might also be mute.

Remember the politeness paralysis that infected me and other wealthy little white girls in charm school? It actually seems pretty inconsequential in the grand scheme of things. Charm School certainly isn't a microcosm of society, but I've come to think that those overt lessons from childhood to speak only in pleasantries reveal the same covert doctrine pervasive in much of white America. We do not speak of injustices. It is the manifesto that unites us, a silence of the privileged.

In their book *Wiser: Getting Beyond Groupthink to Make Groups Smarter*, authors Cass R. Sunstein and Reid Hastie present the danger of groups that have no dissenting voice within their ranks to question or disturb the status quo. They speak of "happy talk"[69] as the banter within such groups that reassures members that all is well. I was raised on it. Sunday dinner conversations always included, "We're just so blessed, so fortunate." Now I wonder if under the guise of happy chatter were the chords of another message: "Thank God we aren't them. We're sorry for them, but no one can hold us responsible; it's just the way it is. We're blessed." And there you have it. We recognize inequalities but don't speak of them. We're grateful we're on the right side of the fence, or the tracks, or sitting in the front of the bus.

But, of course, we did speak about the "Negros" and sometimes the "Nigs," all the dire warnings about keeping the neighborhood safe, our family pure. But it seemed more like background noise, less distinct than the message that we were good people who didn't see color and certainly weren't racist. Ironically, those negative racial messages really were white noise, background sound that seemed almost inaudible.

If I sound confused, I am. I still really don't understand how it worked, how I could live with such divergent racial messages without being aware of the hypocrisy. All I know is it was real. Sociologist Stanley Cohen captured it well, writing, "Denial may be neither a matter of telling the truth nor intentionally telling a lie. There seem to be states of mind, or even whole cultures, in which we know and deny at the same time."[70] That was the culture I called home.

I knew we weren't racists. And I knew we were.

My student Nathan and I were raised in this culture. At some level of consciousness, we knew we were living in a system of racial inequality, but it just didn't seem to be wrong—for us. Plato and Malcolm X knew what we needed: others who would challenge us to question.

There were African Americans in my childhood. The fleeting appearance of a black babysitter, a few who worked at the country club, bellhops in hotels carrying our luggage, and one maid my mom employed for a short while. Certainly, no one black joined us at the dining room table. We may have watched the then-controversial film *Guess Whose Coming to*

Dinner (1967), in which Sidney Poitier played the black fiancé coming home to meet the very white parents of Spencer Tracy and Audrey Hepburn, but that was entertainment, not reality.

There were some black students in college, a few colleagues when I began teaching, and students I saw in the hallway but rarely in my classroom. Encountering *others* remained an exception rather than a common occurrence. And when you are raised on the divergent messages of "race doesn't matter," and "avoid black people," it was almost accurate to say I didn't notice them–until I crossed the hallway to teach African American Literature. Ironically, while I knew black students took the course, I was still somehow surprised to *see* them there. I was alone, a minority for the first time in my life. There were a whole lot of *others*.

Two myths from my upbringing in The Land of Only White deserted me quite quickly. I had been taught to say I didn't even see color. That was the polite and appropriate thing to say. But it was a lie: here were thirty black students looking at my singular white face. And I had been taught that regardless of skin, we were all the same. It didn't take me long to know I was in new territory, immersed in a culture that was not my own.

Once, one of my African American students lost her mother. I wanted to pay my respects and attend the funeral. Walking into the church, I found myself scanning the congregation for another white face. A new experience—I never felt the need to look for whites in public before; there were always plenty of them there.

When I found none, I squeezed myself into a pew next to the oldest African American woman I could find. She sat shriveled, hunched over her cane. I had heard that sometimes things got "lively" in an African American church, in stark contrast to the silence I knew in my own. I reasoned that surely this elderly lady couldn't move and would stay quiet. I was safe beside her.

Bad choice: when the preacher began, up she rose shouting right back at him, "Praise the Lord." How did such a small, old body house such a booming voice? And it got worse. When the music began, she went to rocking, swaying, and singing, loudly. What did she need that cane for? I sat next to her, frozen white.

I wish all of us residing in The Land of Only White could experience being in the minority for an extended period of time. The learning would be immense. You're finally out of the echo chamber. Without the voices of your own, you begin to hear from others. It's harder to count on your rightness when you are outnumbered. You've left the cave and traveled to a new land—I just don't think many will sign up for the trip.

Another Kind of Other: Books

Regina entered my class for the first time in the middle of a discussion about students' personal reading histories. I had asked them to think about what books had influenced them. Often repeated in their words were the memories of parents reading bedtime stories they never tired of: *Good Night Moon* and *Charlotte's Web*. Some explained that they had enjoyed books until teachers got hold of them, assigning boring texts that meant nothing to them, ones they were forced to read and forced to value only for a grade on a test: *Animal Farm, The Scarlett Letter*, and *Great Expectations*. Some of their titles made me cringe; apparently, I was a contributing culprit.

A counselor escorted Regina in, announcing to the class that we had a new student. To me, she whispered only two words, "She's homeless." I would like to write that I didn't know what to think of that information, but apparently, I did. My mind began formulating a picture of her life, and it didn't include books. As she took a seat and began to grasp what we were talking about, I made the decision not to put her on the spot. I didn't want to embarrass her. Surely a homeless child didn't have a parent who read to her or books lining the shelves of her home. And I quickly came to the assumption that she probably wasn't a very strong reader. All these thoughts came in the instant of two words, "She's homeless." I felt I knew Regina without ever speaking to her. Apparently, in my world *homeless* aligned with illiterate.

But Regina's hand went up. She wanted to contribute. "I'm not sure you'll understand this," she said looking directly at me, "but my family has had to move quickly; we've…had to move in a hurry. Whenever this happens, the first thing my mother yells is, "*Go get the books*!""

It took her words for me to realize how fast a mind reaches for its file cabinet of stereotypes. Regina slammed that mental drawer shut. She became one of my strongest students. She was already an excellent reader when she came into class, but I have to wonder if she hadn't spoken up that first day, would I have continued to judge and even overlook her? Would I have been able to *see* Regina?

I needed Regina to show me how quickly I put stock in stereotypes instead of investing in an individual. Many of us in The Land of Only White need her mother to yell at us, "Go get the books!" We need to honor them the way she did. We need to recognize their value and their power.

Even if we aren't ready to change our residence from The Land of Only White to experience being the minority, we still have a chance to expand our boundaries. Books can manifest the minds of authors who don't look or think like us. They come from another land. They can serve as a representative of Plato's enlightened other leading the way to freedom beyond our limited thought.

Malcolm X knew this literally. Serving seven years in prison, he wrote:

> Anyone who has read a great deal can imagine the new world that opened. Let me tell you something: from

> then until I left that prison, in every free moment I had, if I was not reading, in the library, I was reading in my bunk. You couldn't have gotten me out of books with a wedge…months passed without my even thinking about being imprisoned. In fact, up to then, I never had been so truly free in my life.[71]

Reading served as an escape, a kind of tunnel into the fresh air of momentary freedom. But books can do more than transport us temporarily; they have the potential to transform us permanently. Books led him not only out of the darkness of a prison cell but also helped free him from an American system of injustice that attempted to claim him—literally and mentally. He emerged a free man who had the power to recreate his life.

With access to libraries, technology that allows us to hold hundreds of manuscripts in the palm of our hand, and books lining the shelves of our homes, books abound in The Land of Only White. Their abundance makes it easier for us to take them for granted, to forget their potential to enlighten, to educate. This kind of reading requires suspending personal beliefs to fully consider the mind of the writer, the other. A process of reflective questioning should follow the reading. As philosopher and educator Mortimer J. Adler explains,

> That is exactly what reading a book should be: a conversation between you and the author. Presumably he knows more about the subject than you do; naturally, you'll have the proper humility as you approach him. But don't let anybody tell you that a reader is supposed

> to be solely on the receiving end. Understanding is a two way operation; learning doesn't consist in being an empty receptacle. The learner has to question himself and question the teacher. He even has to argue with the teacher, once he understands what the teacher is saying.[72]

Then the readers must ask if they can stand firm in their previous assumptions or must they revise based on the new perspective offered? This kind of meeting of the minds, the author and reader's, demands we never be so sure of ourselves that our beliefs can't be altered. It requires the "flexibility of mind" that Malcolm X said was essential to all who say they believe in education. We need the *other* books, the ones that should provoke intelligent self-examination.

Recently a neighbor came to visit. Bryan Stevenson's book, *Just Mercy*, lay bookmarked on the table. She picked it up, saying casually, "What's it about? Is it good?"

I paused. "Well, it's about our messed-up judicial system. It may be one of the most depressing books I've ever read."

Her immediate response: "Then why are you reading it?"

I would love to say I had a profound response, something about the need to educate myself, but instead, I just shrugged. Long after she left I sat there with the book in my lap, not opening it. The book upset me. I could only read small passages at a time and always left it disturbed. Why continue? Stevenson's stories of the innocent unfairly incarcerated, of youth who grow old and die in prison, of death row inmates who smell the burning flesh of those being electrocuted, of a judicial system that favors the white and wealthy—why did I want to know this? I didn't feel like an educator, only tired and very old. And that's when I remembered Dorothy.

Dorothy, far from Kansas and lost in the land of Oz, placed her trust in the great and powerful Wizard. She traveled to find him, believing he would grant her wish to return home. But she discovered Oz was not a deity but only a flawed and feeble old man capable of great deception. I always respected Dorothy for pulling back the curtain, for exposing the painful truth. That's why we must read. Truth demands this even when we risk losing the illusions that have comforted us.

Of course, *The Wizard of Oz* is a beautiful children's tale. I want it rewritten for adults with a darker ending. Grown up Dorothy should not be allowed to click her heels and return home. She should remain lost and looking. New knowledge is always disorienting when we are displaced into an uncharted territory of new understanding. Being lost is not being blind, but instead the first step in gaining vision. It is the imbalance, the discomfort, needed to pursue the truths we may not want to know.

Ta-Nehisi Coates writes that as an African American, "education was a kind of discomfort, was the process that would not award me my own especial Dream but would break all the dreams, all the comforting myths of Africa, of America, and everywhere, and would leave me only with humanity in all its terribleness."[73] He recognized that being in school does not equate with education, reflecting "I sensed the schools were hiding something, drugging us with false morality so that we would not see, so that we did not ask....Schools did not reveal truths, they concealed them."[74]

I was not as perceptive as Coates. For the most part, what I learned in my years of being a white student in white public schools kept me blind and content. The truth of America's injustices and inequities were *white*washed in my formal education. My schooling had not prepared me to teach African American Literature, but when I began reading African American writers and historians, when I read from the perspective of an *other*, my education began. For the first time I had to question my previous understandings.

A Hallway

It's amazing what I now see when standing in a school hallway. From this vantage point, I see America's strengths and weaknesses, its broken promises and potential. Its strengths? Forever and always our youth, in all their beautiful restlessness. I will never agree with those who say teenagers have changed for the worse. Thirty-four years I have watched them grow. They are the same amazing beings as always, not less respectful or lacking a work ethic or any of the criticisms wielded at them. They are kids. And if you find one rude or unruly, they are only a mirror of the adults who have raised them. They emerge as their true selves when given the chance.

America's weakness? We are a nation in need of education. Both sides of the achievement gap are deficient. On one side of the hall, we see the obvious needs of those who most often reside on the bottom. Low literacy rates and weak test scores confirm their status. It comes as no surprise that illiteracy and crime are closely related. The Department of Justice states the link between academic failure and delinquency, violence, and crime is fused to reading failure. Two thirds of students who cannot read proficiently by the end of 4th grade will end up in jail or welfare. Nearly 85 percent of the juveniles who face trial in juvenile court are functionally illiterate. Over 70 percent of inmates in America's prisons cannot read above a fourth grade level. And one in four children in America grow up without learning how to read.[75] A recent article from the Huffington Post summarized it well: "Economic security, access to health care, and the ability to actively participate in civil life all depend on an individual's ability to read."[76]

Research tells us that two-thirds of U.S. high school students struggle to comprehend what they are reading, and I know these students. In the struggle, many give up the battle. I remember proctoring the SAT, the standardized test used to determine college readiness. Reading skills are essential to survive the lengthy test. So is stamina. Five minutes into the exam, I watched three students pull their hoods up over their heads and settle in for a long morning nap. All of them could read, but at the first roadblock in their understanding, they gave up. Sleep seemed a better use of time. They looked exhausted and weak.

But I now think there is also a less apparent weakness in the reading ability in many of the students who reside on the other side of the hall—a weakness of the mind. In this group we deem as scholars, education has often been diminished to a celebration of grades and test scores. School has become the business of getting into college. Succeeding in school does not guarantee an "intelligent search for truth." Students, instead, are often on an intelligent pursuit of grades. Plagiarism and cheating abound, not because these successful students are intrinsically more dishonest, but because they have adopted strategies of survival in the competitive realm they find themselves in. We tell them they are the valued students, brighter than the others. They feel pressured not to disappoint.

Let me tell you of Mary, a petite sophomore girl who sat

pensively waiting for me to pass back her quiz. When she saw that she had received a B, she collapsed into tears. Between sobs, I heard her fear. "Now I'll never get into medical school." Let me tell you of Phillip, the smartest student I ever had, who shot himself in his senior year when West Point denied his admission. Love of learning has left these students replaced by a fear of failure so strong it drives them to doubt their own minds. When reading academic texts their ability to question is reduced to, "Will be on the test?" not "What do I actually think? How does this material affect me?" Reading allowed Malcolm X to transform his future. Some, like Phillip, can't see a future at all. Students on both sides of the achievement gap and both classrooms I stand between, Honors English and African American Literature, are in need of education.

Both need reading lessons.

Systems of oppression are far easier to sustain when people aren't reading. Why else was it a crime to teach a slave to read? The illiterate are easier to oppress. Frederick Douglass, who began life as a slave himself, stated "Once you learn to read you will be forever free."[77] I'm sure he would see our present-day system of educational inequities that holds so many African American students on the bottom of the achievement gap as nothing less than a continuation of the servitude he experienced.

But I now believe that many white students we call scholars are also oppressed. Trying furiously to survive the expectations for academic success we have put on them, we have reduced them to talented test takers not critical thinkers who have the power to determine their own paths. It was

Malcolm X who said, "The most important thing we can do today is learn to think for ourselves."[78] Systems of oppression can only fall when both the oppressed and the oppressor have the courage of independent thought.

What the view from the hallway most confirms for me is that we are a divided nation. Standing between the classroom doors of Honors English and African American Literature I see the divide. By race, by economics, and by an achievement gap determined to maintain a system of inequity, both groups of students are harmed by this divide. Both are blinded by a societal lie of their determined value and worth. Neither is free.

And neither was I. I taught for years before realizing what my high school was teaching me. Students don't only learn the disciplines of English, history, math, and science. The school itself also teaches students a curriculum on race, and it's overt and covert messages comprise the same double-sided racial education in which I was indoctrinated. My high school is a microcosm of American society. By studying it, I have learned much of what imprisons so many of us in The Land of Only White.

My school crafted a vision statement so the public could know what we believe. It is written on the school's website and showcased on the school walls. It reads:

> [We are]… a diverse and inclusive school community. We are committed to developing academic excellence, integrity, and independent thinkers who are life-long learners devoted to good citizenship and to celebrating diversity and equity. Students will graduate prepared

to excel as caring and productive global citizens.[79]

No wonder I am proud to work in this school. It reads like a vision of America itself. No wonder I am proud to be an American. But once again, what we profess and practice in both school and society are often in discord. Reality does not support the vision.

Think of Plato's prisoners, "their legs and necks so fastened that they can only look straight ahead of them and cannot turn their heads."[80] It seems incredulous that they don't know they are chained. Can't they feel the shackles on their legs and the weight about their necks? But they know nothing else, and their vision remains one-dimensional. They trust the insubstantial shadows. Freedom can only occur when they question if there is any substance of truth within those shadows. Freedom from The Land of Only White came only when I began to question the myths I was raised to trust.

I didn't know the word *equivocate* until Shakespeare taught it to me while I was reading *The Tragedy of Macbeth*. The witches equivocate to Macbeth, deceiving him with veiled promises. He begins the play a humble man, but the witches' well-crafted half-truths lead him to believe he will be more than mortal. He will rule over all, a King that "no man born of woman"[81] can kill. Macbeth's trust in these equivocations cost him dearly: he loses his head. And that's what I think has happened to many of us in the Land of Only White. We've lost our heads, too. Trusting the equivocations we have been raised on, we believe in our own superiority while remaining blind to the systemic inequities that prevent others from usurping our power. Shakespeare's play begins with the words,

"Fair is foul, and foul is fair."[82] How closely this parallels my student's words about racism in America: "It might not be fair, but it's right." I had to carefully examine America's equivocations, and my school provided me the text.

The Equivocation of Integration

AMERICA SAYS IT BELIEVES in integration. In *Brown v The Board of Education* (1954) the Supreme Court declared separate schools for black and white children unconstitutional, but American schools remain more separated by race than ever. My own high school prides itself in its diversity while practicing separation every day. And separate remains unequal. White and black students find themselves in classrooms predominantly filled with their own. In advance placement and honors courses, white students make up the vast majority. Black students can be found in regular and basic courses. The course titles themselves reveal what the school denies. We tell the public that we do not believe in tracking students on any academic path. A student can choose to take any course, can choose to excel. But reality dispels this myth. The track you begin as a freshman (honors, regular, or basic) will likely be the track you remain in as a senior. It's possible to change, but odds are you won't. Many factors contribute to the unacknowledged but very real tracking system. Counselors, often with the best of intentions, will help students pick their classes, warning them this one might be too difficult, or you might be more comfortable here. Students also self-select, often choosing to remain in their same track to be with friends, to remain comfortable. And if students do challenge themselves to take higher-level courses, the teacher may be confused as to how to help the student excel when they aren't coming to the class with the same skills as those who have remained in honors courses. Then it is the teacher who is uncomfortable. Comfort does not produce academic excellence, but it does perpetuate the achievement gap that helps ensure black and white students will continue to live in different worlds when they leave our institution, just as they did within it.

My school and my country say they celebrate diversity and equity, but the disparity between races goes far beyond academics. America the melting pot? We only ask minorities to do the melting.

One small assignment helped me see this truth. I administered two identical quizzes in Honors English and African American Literature. The first contained questions such as:

What was the brown paper bag test used for?

Who was Sally Hemings?

Who was Emmett Till?

What are chitterlings?

On average, how often do African America women wash their hair?

When white students perused the page, there was outright protest. "Does this count for a grade?"

"This isn't fair."

"How would I know this?"

"*Why* would I know this?"

In African American Literature, students got to work without concern.

Then I passed out the second quiz containing questions like:

What is the SAT?

Who was Christopher Columbus?

Who was Thomas Jefferson?

What is escargot?

On average, how often do white women wash their hair?

White students still wanted to know if it counted for a grade, but they began writing answers confidently and without complaint. Black students did the same.

African America students passed both tests; white students only their own.

I realize how often a woman washes her hair seems inconsequential, but what the quiz revealed was black students know a lot about white history and white behavior. On the other hand, whites students not only don't know about black people, they don't feel they need to. If we believe we honor integration in America because black and white students attend the same school, we are mistaken. Black students navigate two cultures while white students remain in the dark (or is it the white?) when it comes to African American culture.

It makes me think of a field trip my students and I took to the African American History Museum in Detroit, Michigan. It has an exhibit of a slave ship. You descend a dark staircase into the bowels of the vessel. There you see the misery and pain kidnapped Africans endured. This is our white history, too. The Europeans attempted to deceive themselves of the horror by the names they gave slave ships: *Jesus*, *Good Hope*, *Friendship*.... We do the same by labeling it African American history, but it is an equivocation, a lie, if we do. We were there. It is American history.

Remember the well-intending counselors who may dissuade African American students from taking higher-level courses? Once a white student told me when he went to pick his courses for the following school year, he asked his counselor to include African American Literature. She immediately responded, "Why would you want to take that? It would be too easy for you." He took the course anyway and reported back to her of the academic challenges he faced in this course. This woman did not know the curriculum; she had never sat in my classroom. Why is it she believed it would be too easy? Why is it she wondered if he would want to learn about African American Literature and history? Was it because she could not imagine herself being interested in the course? In a school and country that celebrates diversity, why would he not want to take the class?

I also remember when I was going on maternity leave and needed another teacher to take over the course for a semester. When no teachers volunteered, my department chairman said she would do it. She asked for me to present my lesson plans and reading lists for her to review in order to prepare. She came back in a couple days perplexed, telling me: "I don't know this stuff. I didn't realize it would take so much work to prepare." This white teacher was the head of the English department. She taught Humanities and made it known she was a member of the intellectual elite. Her own education had been very white, and so were the students she taught in my diverse high school. She asked the only African American male in the English Department to take over the course.

Integration doesn't mean you have to serve chitlins at your

Thanksgiving dinner or celebrate Kwanzaa in addition to Christmas. I am suggesting what poet Langston Hughes asked for back in 1965. He said we must accept that there has been no integration in America and attempt a "reintegration."[83] Reintegration would require all citizens to learn a little and respect a lot about one another. It doesn't require the majority to study every minority extensively, but it means acknowledging ignorance rather than casting judgment against what you don't understand. When we in The Land of Only White ask, "Why do *they* act that way, or dress like that, or speak like that?" we aren't asking questions that seek understanding. Instead we are delivering veiled statements of disrespect that reinforce our preferred separation.

The Equivocation of Meritocracy

We, in The Land of Only White, have been taught that hard work is what counts in America. Those who rise to the top do so because of effort, not privilege; will power, not wealth. We believe, regardless of race or social status, you can rise to any height. Meritocracy is America's creed.

We offer up our rags to riches stories to prove meritocracy is no lie: Fredrick Douglas, and W.E.B. Du Bois, Oprah Winfrey and Ben Carson. Malcolm X himself stands as evidence. These exceptions are real, but they also serve to deceive. Because some individuals defeat the odds does not mean the system is sound.

Competition drives us to be at the top, to be the winner. It makes me think about musical chairs. Most remember playing the game as a kid, but you'd be surprised at how excited teenagers can be to play it again in a classroom. Even those who have mastered disinterest can't resist. I line up chairs, one less than the number of students and put on some music. Students glide past seats, hips swaying and voices singing to the old Motown hits I usually play.

But when the music stops, the game turns competitive as students dive for chairs. Another is removed, and the music resumes. Initially, the students who can't find a seat reluctantly accept their fate. They are out of the game. But as the number of chairs declines, the intensity increases. Bodies slam into one another dashing for the dwindling seats. Sweaty students complain that the classroom has turned into a stinky gym locker room, but no one wants to stop. Always, near the end, I scream not to run, not to hurt anyone, and I wonder why I ever play this game. When the music ends for the last time. there is a sole winner sitting on the final chair. The other competitor is often on the floor. One year, a student jumped on top of his seat screaming, "I am the winner!" Competition at its finest.

Then I tell students we're going to play a different version of the game. In this rendition, chairs are still eliminated, but not people. When the music stops, students still move to an open chair, but it there isn't one, they must ask to share a seat or a lap. Rather than one lone winner on one lone chair as in the traditional game, this one ends with thirty students balancing each other on the final seat.

When I describe the game, many tell me it is impossible, but I know it's not. It does, however, require thought and effort to make it happen. As the chairs become scarce, bigger students usually volunteer to sit first, and then strategically, others begin placing themselves, balancing on someone's knee. Lightweight students are often held on a precarious pile of bodies. When all are successfully on the single seat, I make them hold their position long enough to take their picture. Then they collapse in laughter. No one was eliminated; they have completed a feat they didn't believe was possible.

Now the discussion begins. "Why did we play both of these versions of musical chairs? What might they represent in the real world? What are they *really* about?"

Students moan. "Why do we always have to think about

things?" (I never grow tired of this complaint.) With only a little prodding, students draw parallels between the games and society.

"The first is like America…everyone out for themselves," one student ventures.

"Yeah, that's what capitalism is all about…and it's how school is. We compete for grades to get into college, to get money….to win!"

Now someone contemplates, "The second is kind of like socialism or something. Everyone's the same; no one winner."

When I ask, "Which did you personally prefer?" responses vary. Students are clear when I pose, "What would a classroom look like if it was based on the second game?"

"We wouldn't compete against each other. We'd help each other…and everyone would get the same grade."

I suggest we try that second method, of everyone helping each other and then giving them all the same grade, perhaps the average of all their test scores, and they are equally clear. "No way! That wouldn't be fair. I don't want what everyone else gets. Someone would mess me up. I want my A."

When it comes to personal preference, I can't choose. I value the implications of each game. Both require individual effort, but the second version depends upon something more, on group support, and it requires a lot of work from all members. You try balancing thirty students on one chair. A seeming impossibility, it can be done.

In overcrowded classrooms, teachers have been doing this delicate balancing act for decades. In the game, chairs are taken away, and in reality, classroom resources grow scarce. Students literally may have to share seats. I have had several classes where the number of students outnumbered desks.

But the second game's real significance lies in its figurative meaning. Students are embraced, not eliminated. All work together toward a common goal, to see and grasp education's power to change lives. We need to support one another to make sure we are all well equipped to face the struggles outside the classroom. It is a challenge that places responsibility on all its members.

The traditional game of musical chairs is about competition. Offering only one winner; the rest are out. A comparison with our society is certainly possible: only some win; others feel like losers. If the chairs represent opportunity to stay in the game, many feel they have had them pulled out from beneath them. Some don't even see the chair or opportunity directly in front of them until it's too late. However, that's not the only parallel I see.

Most students like the traditional game of musical chairs. Even with the knowledge that the odds of winning are slim, most want to play. It's exciting to see how far you can get in the game. And that's what I hope students take with them: the real world won't offer you a lap to sit on, but it should offer you the possibility of success. Individual effort and hard work should get you further. If we played by the rules and didn't steal chairs, there is nothing wrong with competition.

If we played by the rules.

It brings me back to my student Nathan's summary on racial inequality in America, "It might not be fair, but it's right." Playing by the rules is fair, but for many, it doesn't feel right. America's rules aren't colorblind. For black Americans, playing fair doesn't prevent you from being marginalized and overlooked. And for many white people, playing by the rules seems fair, as long as the unstated ones give us the advantage. I want to believe in America's meritocracy because it allows me to see my success as mine alone. I now see through the equivocation.

In The Land of Only White we practice an Orwellian understanding of equality. As George Orwell wrote in *Animal Farm*, "All animals are equal, but some animals are more equal than others."[84] White Americans have the *more* when it comes to equality: more opportunities in education, in careers, in financial success. The list goes on and the *more* gives you the advantage. You still have to work hard, but the system of meritocracy is fundamentally flawed in our favor.

THE EQUIVOCATION OF POWER

ANIMAL FARM WAS ORWELL'S CRITIQUE and criticism of the Russian Revolution, but its implication extends to any system of power and oppression. Power has the inherent potential to corrupt, and those in power do not want to lose their position. Power is something you fight for and once it is attained, you try to hold on to it. It's an all-or-nothing kind of thing. To lose power would be just that: to lose. And in the competitive Land of Only White we don't like losers.

We can't conceive of sharing power with others.

Plato had a very different concept, writing "...what we need is that the only men to get power should be men who do not love it."[85] He believed education was the essence of an individual's power. An enlightened one didn't try to withhold power from others; he only attempted to show a way out of ignorance. The prisoners of the cave still had to choose to walk on their own two feet. Living twenty-four hundred years later, Malcolm X embodied Plato's philosophy, choosing to educate himself within his prison cell. He transformed his life, and wanted others to do the same. A powerful leader, he did not seek to rule over others but to inspire them to find their own power. He was considered a master teacher.

Many of us are not master teachers when it comes to encouraging students to find their own power. In fact, we are equivocators. Educators often talk about empowering students while denying them power in their own classrooms.

When I began teaching, only a few years of age separated me from the teenagers who sat before me. They weren't sure they could take me seriously. They seemed to like me, but when I asked them to get to work, it felt like a test of wills—mine against theirs. I worried I would lose the battle and sought advice from some sympathetic and seasoned colleagues. I remember what one told me in particular: "Don't smile until Christmas. You aren't there to be their friend. Write down a list of all your rules and tell them what will happen if they break them. You're the boss."

That night I typed up my new laws, two pages of them, which I passed out to students the next day. I presented all the potential consequences, the threats and punishments I was prepared to deliver if I didn't have their respect. They were going to take me seriously now. It was the traditional model of power and control that had governed my own schooling. My students were familiar with it. For them, it was business as usual, and I was even able to smile before the holidays. I never thought to question the merits of this system of control or the underlying lesson I was teaching my students.

Ron Ritchhart, in his book *Creating Cultures of Thinking*, examines both the overt and covert messages we send every day in classrooms, many in opposition with each other. While promising to empower youth, Ritchhart says the traditional teacher often remains the authoritarian expert who tells "students what to think, not how to think." Instead of discovering their own abilities for critical thought, this traditional methods of instruction "distance students from their own ideas, opinions, creativity, and reason."[86]

"We dispense knowledge; bring your own container."

Educator Martin Haberman recounts seeing this banner hanging over the doors of an urban high school. Hung with pride, Haberman believes it reveals the traditional model of education that has actually served to diminish learning and weaken students.[87] In the early years of my career, it could have hung in my classroom. Empowering students meant pouring *my* knowledge into them. After all, stuck in Plato's cave with my lofty credentials, I saw myself as one of the enlightened ones. It was my job to pour.

I now see that in that paradigm, I was the only one required to think. Students needed to memorize what I said. I was producing successful mimics, but not critical thinkers. If I wanted something different, the entire structure had to change. I began to think about what relinquishing some of my control might look like.

It looked like a big, red, rubber ball.

Standing in front of the classroom today, I hold that ball. I tell my students to imagine that it represents all the knowledge that I have. It's my ball. To get that knowledge they need to stare at it—in effect, at me—while remaining quiet for the whole hour. They look at me like I've lost my mind.

I tell them, "This is how I remember school when I was growing up. The teacher or professor had the knowledge. My job was to listen and take it in. A student was not to disturb the instructor."

Now I throw the ball to one student and ask him to throw it back to me. I hold it for a while and then throw it to another, who promptly returns it to me. "When I first began teaching, this is how it was. I had the knowledge, but students could ask questions and contribute. Still, all eyes remained on me; students spoke only to me. Make no mistake; it was still *my* ball.

Now, I throw it to a student and that student throws it to another; someone else asks for the ball. It sails around from student to student, finally coming back to me. Holding it briefly, I send it out again. "This is what I want a classroom to look like now."

Students get the point. All hands need to be on that ball, their fingerprints marking its surface. As active members of the classroom, we all need to stretch to receive not only my knowledge but the knowledge each student possesses. Knowledge needs to be seen as something fluid and evolving, not a finite box (or in this case, ball) of wisdom that the teacher owns. It means I can no longer see myself as the sole expert and my students as mere containers. I have to enter into a relationship of shared power.

LOST

Shared Power

A CULTURE OF SHARED POWER in the classroom meant a redefinition of myself as an educator. Of course, I would still be the one most in charge. Shared power does not connote chaos. It is the educator's ultimate responsibility to keep students safe and focused on the learning. But the titles of authoritarian and expert had to go. I had to get out of the spotlight and let students share the stage. Educational reformer Jawanza Kunjufu helped me with this redefinition when he said to consider where a coach stands: out of center and on the sidelines with his team.

Kunjufu identifies six types of teachers, ranking them from worst to best. Worst is the custodian who puts in his time and counts down days till retirement; then the referral agent, seeking always to reduce his load by transferring students to special education classes or out the door in suspensions; next the missionary, coming to convert others to his way of business, oblivious to cultural differences; then the instructor who teaches his subject but does not feel responsible for students learning; Kunjufu recognizes next the master teacher, knowledgeable in both his subject and learning styles. But it is the coach who stands above all. He not only merges pedagogy and learning styles—most significantly, he cultivates a bond with his students. Kunjufu believes, "You cannot teach a child you do not respect, love, or understand."[88]

Some might say these goals of respect, love, and understanding sound more appropriate for summer camp than a classroom. Too much *kumbaya* and not enough academic rigor. Others might challenge Kunjufu to teach in their school. How can you expect teachers to respect, love, or understand the disengaged and sometimes enraged students who sit in overcrowded classrooms? Kunjufu believes we can't afford not to. Good coaches love more than the game; they respect their individual players and cultivate the concept of team. A teacher, as coach, believes in education, in hard work, and in unifying his students into battle to emerge as victors, as scholars of critical thought.

You can't learn a sport by sitting on the bench all day listening to lectures. A coach models his expertise, but the athlete must also be allowed to move, make some noise, make mistakes, and attempt to score on their own. Of course there is a time for drills, repetitions, and practice. My daughters all played high school basketball; there were hours of dribbling down the court, shooting free throws, and doing suicide drills to increase endurance. They may not have liked it, but they didn't see it as unimportant. They gave it all they had, knowing the goal was not the drill but the game. There, players move in creative plays and spontaneous movement. They feel their own power.

In the classroom, there is a place for rote learning, memorization, practice, and even an occasional lecture. There is a time for teachers to impart their knowledge as students learn addition and subtraction, times tables, the elements of the periodic table, literary terms, and the seven continents. But let teachers emulate coaches. The instruction must actively involve students, and the intent must be more than mastery of material for the upcoming test. The goal must be for students to exercise their own creative power of critical thought in the classroom and in the real-life game beyond the school's walls. They must be allowed to consider and disagree, question and reconsider. They must be allowed to formulate their own thoughts. Instead of giving them our answers, educators need to teach students the skills to find their own.

The students who sit before us now turn to the Internet for instant knowledge. Type in any question and, without effort or thought, the answer will appear. But this is not reality. The world will demand they struggle through complex problems that have no immediate solutions. *Should I marry? Should I divorce? Should I take this career path or choose another? How do I handle illness or cope with the death of a loved one? Where do I stand on the complex issues in society? Do I believe in God?* These questions cannot be handed to computer-generated responses. Instant answers do not make us wise. The ability to question, the skill to synthesize information, the artistry to craft our own understanding: this makes us wise. We need to give students the tools of critical thinking and the space to hone their skills. Thinking is hard work. Good coaches and good teachers demand it.

Hard work: we're back to the sacred ethic in The Land of Only White. So often I hear my fellow teachers—the vast majority in America being white—reiterating the same complaint: "My students just won't do the work."

We need to start by asking ourselves what is this *work* we are asking them to do? I used to resent it when students asked, "Why do we need to do this?" It seemed like whining. Now, I think it is a legitimate question that deserves an answer. And if we don't have one or all we can say is, "It will be on the test," we need to step back and evaluate our motives. Students know the difference between *work* and *busy work.* Busy work is designed to pass time but in and of itself has little or no value. It is a tool of control to keep students occupied, quiet, and passive.

The class discussion focused on the character of Mr. Dalton from *Native Son.* A white and wealthy real estate mogul who donates thousands of dollars to Negro College Funds, he also segregates black people into the worst rental areas of Chicago. During the discussion I called on Leon to weigh in on this complex character. His response was unexpected: "I don't know yet. No teacher ever asked me real questions." I told him to keep thinking and let us know when he wanted to offer his ideas.

After class, I asked him to tell me about those "real questions." He was clear, "You're asking me to really think. I'm used to questions like: 'Where does Mr. Dalton live? What does Mr. Dalton do for a living? What is the name of Mr. Dalton's cat?'"

There is nothing inherently wrong with those questions. They can be used to check for reading comprehension. Some teachers tell me they ask only these questions so students can experience success. They can get their A. But if these are the only kind of questions we ask of students, we have taught them far more than a cat's name. Leon had learned his teachers did not believe he was able to handle the real questions, that he was not capable of critical thought.

Leon was smart enough to know his teachers were wrong.

He knew he was capable, but other students succumb to the teacher's implicit message that they'll never be as smart as those kids who sit across the hall in honors classes. They, like the classes they find themselves in, are "regular" or "basic" or "lower level." And then we wonder why they don't seem interested in learning. They do not feel empowered; they feel resigned to a state of mind they can't control. They know they will never succeed academically and aren't expected to. They fulfill the label.

The recent work of Stanford University psychologist Carol Dweck insists we must teach students the power of their own brains. Years of researching motivation, on what makes some people successful and others not, has brought her to the concept of what she terms "mindset."

> In a fixed mindset students believe their basic abilities, their intelligence, their talents, are just fixed traits. They have a certain amount and that is that....In a growth mindset students understand that their talents and abilities can be developed through effort, good teaching, and persistence. They don't necessarily think everyone is the same or anyone can be Einstein, but they believe everyone can get smarter if they work at it.[89]

The brain, like a good muscle, actually grows when it is exercised. When students believe they have the ability to increase their intellectual power, they will accept the work it requires. Their efforts produce results and have worth. If, on the other hand, they have been sold a bill of goods that they are not smart and never will be, they will develop strategies to avoid any situation that points out their deficiencies. Remember Rashan, who entertained the class to avoid taking a test? He knew what he was and wanted to keep me from knowing, finally confiding "I don't want you to find out I'm dumb."

If students do not feel worthy of hard work, it is the teacher's job to dispel the lie they have internalized. Maybe one significant individual, a parent or teacher, has made them doubt themselves. In the case of many African American students, it isn't a single individual who has done the damage, but instead a societal message of inferiority. In that case, the teacher must help students understand the conspiracy that has been waged against them so they can access the power of their own brains and embrace the hard work the world will demand of them.

And it isn't enough to just tell students they're capable. We must provide them opportunities to experience their own power for success. When I told Rashan that I knew he was smart, I failed him as an educator. He put no trust in my abstract vision. I needed to provide him concrete proof of his abilities with tasks that would allow him to feel the power of his own success. Then he would have evidence of his intelligence, evidence he could put faith in. So many students are caught in a vicious cycle of failure in our schools. As a colleague once told me, "We educators need to institute a vicious cycle of success."

Almost all teachers will tell you there are moments of brilliance in class discussions or in student writing, sometimes from those you'd least expect. Those moments provide proof of students' power for critical thought. They should not be overlooked or ignored. I now gather these moments of brilliance, printing them out so all students can read, respond, and reflect on the depth of thought offered by their peers. There is something very powerful in seeing your thoughts published. It means you are someone, your voice is acknowledged. It doesn't take long for students to work harder to find their quote on the *Moments of Brilliance Bulletin.* I have seen so many cycles of success begin here. And once again, it's not my thoughts at center stage but their own.

Students were reading a response from Marcus. He had written a comment on a poem we had been studying that I thought was truly original. When students realized the author, several said out loud in disbelief, "Marcus wrote that?" Some turned directly to him astonished: "Wow…you wrote that?" Marcus had previously been defined by his drug-dealing abilities. Now, students saw him in the light of a scholar. Marcus saw himself as a scholar too.

Marcus, like many students, found he was capable of deep, critical thought in discussions, but when it came to a test or written assignment, he still did only enough to get by. Teachers had taught Marcus this expectation. Accepting work that we know is below what a student is capable of reinforces a silent but very clear message: *I will accept very little and not hassle you for more. I will leave you alone, and you will pass.* Then teachers can blame the student: *If that's all he does, this low grade is what he deserves. I can't just give him a good grade for so little.* I agree, but there is another alternative. Break the pattern of mediocrity. Do not accept the work.

I began refusing to accept written work that didn't demonstrate what a student was capable of, and students got mad. I was breaking the rules of school as they had come to know them. I met privately with each student. Almost every conversation was the same:

"It isn't fair; I did the assignment. You *have to* give me credit."

My response was calm and clear: "It would be disrespectful of me to accept this work when I know what you are capable of doing. If you hadn't been so brilliant in class, then maybe I could have taken this poor work as all you were able to do. But now I know. I can accept your anger, but not the assignment until it is completed with the intelligence I saw demonstrated in class discussions." If I had chosen to say this to the class as a whole, I don't think they would have heard my conviction. There may have been a unified revolt. One on one, in the privacy of this conversation, students felt my respect. Most chose to redo the assignment.

Jawanza Kunjufu wrote that this bond of respect between teacher and student is essential for learning. It is this bond that allows me to demand hard work. I sure wouldn't have tried this on the first writing assignment. Trust and respect take time, but once established, students feel their own potential and power. It is a bond of shared power in which both teacher and student recognize each other's strengths and do not settle for less.

This classroom felt very different from the old model I had constructed. Before I prided myself in having cooperative students; they did as I asked. Now I had something beyond cooperation; I had a classroom of collaboration, where students followed not only my expectations for hard work but their own.

I wanted to make sure this culture of collaboration or shared power was evidenced not only by my words and actions but also in the physical classroom itself. Desks were no longer aligned in straight rows where students saw only my face and nothing but the backs of other students' heads. They were arranged so students could see, talk, and listen to each other. I experimented with semi-circles and circles, with paired seats and clusters of four or six. Seating often varied from day to day to allow students different perspectives. And then I started thinking about the walls. How could the walls speak of shared power and an expectation for hard work?

Remember the portraits of all the white, male presidents that lined my school walls as a child? Those walls spoke volumes about who held the power in our country. The walls of my classroom are different now. The first homework I assign students is to bring me a photograph of someone that inspires them to work hard. I enlarge them, displaying them around us. We are surrounded by the eyes of those that motivate them. All of America are depicted here, not a select few.

I don't want students conditioned to believe they work for white, powerful men, or even for me. Their motivation must spring from a source they already trust. Rarely do students choose someone famous. More often it is the eyes of parents and grandparents who line the walls. Sometimes it is a younger sibling for whom they say they are determined to be a good role model. Sometimes it is their own photograph, with the quick explanation, "I don't have anyone. I motivate me." I believe them.

For the second assignment we begin by looking at dedications authors have written for their books. Some make them laugh out loud.

> To my wife Marganit and my children Ella Rose and Daniel Adam without whom this book would have been completed two years earlier.
>
> —Joseph J. Rotman, *An Introduction to Algebraic Topology*

Or the simple but direct:

> This is not for you.
>
> —Mark Z. Danielewski, *House of Leaves*

I remind them that these dedications are published; they are there for anyone to read. I ask them to write a dedication explaining to whom they dedicate this year of hard, academic work. These will also be public, posted around the room. I do make a qualification: if you change your mind during the year, say for example you dedicate it to your boyfriend, but you break up and now think he's a jerk, you are allowed to remove yours from the wall and write a new one.

I remember one in particular. A student wrote:

> I dedicate my year of hard work to my mother. I know we don't get along, and that you think I hate you, but I don't. I really do want to make you proud.

Her mother came in for parent night, read the words, and cried.

I do both assignments also, my picture and dedication posted among theirs. I am a member of the community, not set apart from it. We are all committed to work hard.

I am now convinced that students entrenched in a "just get by" mentality will not embrace academic rigor unless they believe they are a member of a community that values them. It isn't hard to make a parallel with the disenfranchised minorities in America. Why work hard to contribute to a society that doesn't value you? Why not just get by when you will never be allowed to share in the power? Individual respect is a prerequisite of performance not only in a classroom but also in our country.

There's an African riddle I share with students: "A husband and wife were traveling through the jungle. Their respective mothers were with them. All of a sudden, wild beasts began stalking their trail. Tigers and lions hunted them down, wanting to devour them. Together, the frightened four ran to the banks of a river. There was a canoe, their only means of escape. But the vessel would only hold three. The river was broad and deep, filled with crocodiles that thrashed their tails and showed their teeth, hungry for them to enter the water. Any who waded in would meet certain death, and if one remained on shore while the others escaped, a horrible death before the canoe could return was certain. Who should get in the canoe? How should they decide who dies?" Each student writes their answer with a brief explanation of their reasoning. When I have collected the responses, they beg me for the answer. Creating the greatest cliffhanger, I tell them they will have to come to class tomorrow if they want to know the solution. They complain, but I know attendance will be stellar.

Every year their answers make me laugh. I read my favorites out loud the next day, keeping the writers anonymous.

"The oldest mother should die. She's had her life." I remind them that since I'm certainly the oldest, it looks like if we find ourselves on the banks of that river, I'm a goner. Students smile but don't disagree.

"The wife's mother needs to die," a male writes. "I just know my mother-in-law will get on my nerves."

Many say the husband must sacrifice himself. "That's just the way it is; men have to die before women and children." Only a few disagree.

"No way," one student yells. "It's whoever gets in the canoe first. I'd make sure I was in no matter who I had to knock out." He qualifies, "Except not my mom."

They beg for the answer, sure that since I said it was a riddle there must be some trick or play on words that they have missed. But the resolution is as straightforward as it can be: "The unity of the family is the highest priority. The Africans sit down and await death together."

Students are disappointed. Some say it's just plain stupid. This is an old African riddle, I remind them. How might Americans answer it? "Everyone for themselves…they might even kill each other trying to get in the canoe."

This is what I know: many African American students are dying together, literally. Violence claims many. So does poverty. The achievement gap has a death grip on academic futures. Many whites don't mind being the only ones in the canoe. In fact, we own the canoe, leaving others to take their chances with the crocs. We may even express our sadness for those being devoured. "So sorry you're being eaten. So sorry we can't lend a hand." Pity is an emotion of the powerful.

We just can't share the canoe. Our survival depends on it. Here lies the fear I believe takes hold of many in The Land of Only White. What will happen to us if the others overtake us? The Census Bureau tells us that in less than three decades we will no longer be the majority in America. As of 2011 the birth rate of white American babies put us in the minority.[90] The browning of America will make us the new minority. I wonder if we will be interested in sharing power then?

I am always outnumbered in a classroom. There are always more students than me, but relinquishing some of my authority has not lead to chaos or diminished me. The learning has been enriched. I wonder now if this could this be true beyond the boundaries of school? What if learning to share power means we actually become more powerful both in schools and in our country?

Acting Wisely Redefined

STUDENTS OFTEN ASK ME to explain my final rule: Act Wisely. I used to explain it by what it was not, entertaining them with two stories of students who broke the rule and suffered the consequences. One was of an African America girl, I can't remember her name, but I can still see her sitting in the back of the classroom. I could never get her to participate. She often looked at the clock, waiting for the bell to free her not only from her seat but apparently from me also. One day, her hand rose up, and my heart swelled. She was going to join in. I called on her immediately; she offered her thought with certainty: "You're the biggest bitch I know." Students laugh and ask what I did next.

"I threw her out of class."

The second story is of a polite white boy who asked if he could make an appointment with me after school. We scheduled the meeting, and when he appeared at my office door, he asked, "May I close the door?"

"Of course," I said. "What's on your mind?"

And he told me. "I just thought you should know that women should stay at home and not be educators. You just aren't bright enough to be my teacher."

Students don't usually laugh at that one. They gasp, and again want to know what I did.

"I told him to get out."

I shared these stories for years before I realized that in both cases it wasn't just the students who had acted unwisely. I did, too. Throwing students out should never be an educator's first response. Even when difficult, listening and seeking to understand must be first. I'm not saying there's never a time to throw someone out, but it isn't the first, or second, or even third option. If it is, the response only evidences fear of the student or of losing control. I used to believe throwing someone out proved just how powerful I was; now I think it proves the opposite. In The Land of Only White we are often quick to blame others for not following our rules, quick to discard them.

I no longer attempt to define my final classroom rule for students. They will each have to discover what *acting wisely* means to them, but I'm coming to understand what acting wisely demands of me. It means sharing power. I learned the tenets of sharing power within the classroom walls, the changes in my practice allowing both students and me greater freedom to learn. I now believe these same tenets of sharing power are the tools which free me from The Land of Only White.

A Tenet of Shared Power: Listening

Teachers love to talk. We know things. You should listen to us. I don't think teachers are the only ones who feel like that. It might be most adults. After all, we've lived awhile, and we're sure we're right about a thing or two. Many in The Land of Only White feel this way. The need to listen to an *other* just isn't necessary. What is there to learn?

Racial tensions simmer in my high school. Occasionally they flare. Once when they boiled over, the principal appointed another white teacher and me to address the situation. My colleague and I devised our plan to solve the problem. We would bring together a diverse group of students and "teach" them about the damaging effects of discrimination—in one hour. We'd lecture first, asking them to take notes on our wisdom and then allow them to talk during the final minutes of the session. We white teachers thought we could educate students about race from our vast academic understanding and our nearly nonexistent lived experience.

White and black students listened disinterestedly to our words. When we allowed them to speak, they erupted in anger unified by race. The bell rang, signaling the end of class: students moved into the halls ready to fight. Instead of extinguishing tensions, we had brought them to a full burn.

Back in the principal's office, she already knew of our debacle from the commotion in the halls. She asked how we wanted to proceed. My wise colleague said since we had failed miserably, perhaps we needed to stop lecturing and start listening to what the students thought we should do. The principal agreed to carve out of our teaching schedules one period each day to meet with students.

For hours, we remained silent and listened. Repeatedly, black students talked of feeling invisible in school, of feeling like second-class citizens. White students said they didn't understand why black students were so angry. Both knew you couldn't resolve issues in an hour. From their words evolved a new plan: student-lead discussion groups that would meet for five full hours.

We decided we would allow both teachers and students to select our student leaders who would run these meetings. Every school knows you have both positive and negative leaders in a student body. The positive model what we value: academically successful and active in student council, band, or sports. These students have great attendance, are polite to all, and rarely or never serve detentions or suspensions. They are our role models. The other group models the behavior we don't want. Hard to control, they motivate others to disregard school rules and school staff. Often absent in the classrooms, they are a disruptive presence in the hallways. We felt we needed both kinds of leaders. If we were going to hold conversations on issues as potentially combustible as race, we needed all students to feel represented. We needed all voices and all ready to listen.

I will never forget our initial meeting with this selected group of leaders. These representatives of the student population had never found themselves in the same room before.

They didn't know one another and were suspicious of each other and of these two teachers who were telling them they were going to lead school meetings. A local business offered us a space to meet so we could be away from the school campus and the reputations each student held there. We had three days with them, and in that time, they yelled at each other and then began to see what they held in common and where they differed. They learned what being a student in the same building looked like through a new set of eyes. They were the architects of a new program, the CRD, designed to Celebrate and Respect Diversity within the student body. They were our leaders.

They would conduct four meetings a year, inviting a racially diverse group of about sixty students to attend each time. The meetings would last for five hours. Then we asked them to figure out how they were going to facilitate those meetings and what were the outcomes they hoped for. We put it *all* in their hands.

Their plan unfolded: ice-breaker activities would begin the meeting to get students talking. Then they would ask the group to identify what some of the biggest concerns were when it came to their school and the issue of race. They would focus on a few. Next, they would split into smaller groups for students to get to know each other better. After some time, each group would be asked to prepare a skit to demonstrate one of the issues they saw at the school. They would perform this skit in front of the whole group. In the final hour, they would ask what students would be willing to do to help solve some of the issues they had shared during the five hours they had been together.

The student leaders emerged confident in themselves and their plan, but remained skeptical that we, or other school staff, would give them so much power and responsibility. My colleague and I were terrified. We would be present at these meetings but on the sidelines. We promised to try not to get in the way.

The meetings worked. No, they didn't erase all the racial tensions at the school, but they did allow diverse students to hear from different perspectives. Honest conversations broke down many of the barriers students felt because of race. They agreed to small but significant changes: they would acknowledge one another in the hall. Some agreed to have lunch together. Some asked if they could meet after school so they could continue to get to know each other. The student body wanted to be in these sessions; they pleaded to be invited. We repeated these sessions four times a year, hundreds of students eventually participating. Because students were willing to listen to each other, they learned. And so did I.

DWB: I would never have known this acronym before those student-led meetings. When a white male made the statement that racism didn't exist in America anymore, a black male countered with only the reply, "DWB." I had no idea what his response meant. I thought it must be some kind of rebuke, but his retort was explained "Driving while black."

I understood it as racial profiling, but I hadn't given it much thought. And I also knew that while I wouldn't have admitted it, deep down, it sounded like an excuse. If you weren't doing something wrong, why would police pull you over? Most all the black students nodded in agreement that DWB was very real. I doubted it.

If you say, *police* to me, the first word that comes to mind is *help*. As a white woman, I believe they will come to my aid. The association for many of the black students was strikingly opposite. Instead of protecting one from danger, police were often perceived as dangerous in their own right.

After that meeting, I went to a trusted colleague, blurting out simply, "DWB." Her immediate response: "Driving while black. What about it?"

"You believe it?" I questioned. She looked tired, paused, and then asked me a question.

"What do you worry about when your teenage daughters drive?"

"So many things," I answered. "Drunk drivers, or if they drink and get behind the wheel. Using their cell phones and changing music stations instead of concentrating on the road. Breaking down and being stranded…" My list could have gone on.

"Me too," she interrupted. She had a black son, a senior in my class. "What I want to know is, do you go out and check the headlights, the tail-lights, the turn signals nearly every time they drive?" I shook my head, no. I had never done these things.

"My husband and I do. We don't want the police to have a reason to pull him over. We worry about the police and our young black son. Last year, he was driving home from basketball practice when the police pulled him over. They didn't tell him what for but asked for his license. He was in gym shorts and had put his wallet under the seat. When he reached for it, they told him to put his hands up and get out of the car. The police perceived his movement to be a threat that he might be reaching for a gun. He did as he was told and, with hands up, he got out of the car. They spun him around, handcuffed him, and slammed him into a police car. They took him to jail, even when they found the wallet and license under his seat. You might think this is unusual, but it's not."

She got her son out of jail. She had been a lawyer before becoming a teacher and then a counselor. I often needed her guidance. Her story made me think of Brother Umar, of his stories of the police and that "brothers went missing." I don't have to believe either one of them. In fact, if I choose to remain in The Land of Only White, I don't have to even talk to them. But if I do listen, I stand to learn more than the acronym DWB. I can learn of experiences far beyond my boundaries in The Land of Only White.

The CRD Program gained momentum. Students felt there were too few meetings. The school decided to offer a course so the discussions could go deeper on a daily basis. The new class allowed students either English or Social Studies credit as we studied issues related to diversity historically and in the present. Conversation remained at the heart as students discussed the school as a microcosm of society. Other school districts began asking about the program; the student leaders began traveling, conducting meetings with both students and staff in other schools. These schools sought ways to replicate the program in their buildings. But the program met its demise. Examining what ended it reveals much about our problems with the concept of shared power.

It was April 29, 1992. Four white Los Angeles police officers were acquitted after the country had watched them brutally beat black motorist Rodney King. A witness had videotaped the event and released it to the news. Viewers saw the excessive force used by the officers. When they were acquitted, riots broke out in cities across the country. Within our school, teachers and administrators worried what would happen; tensions were high. The principal asked if the student leaders could do something to calm the impending unrest. An announcement was made allowing those who were troubled by the court's verdict to leave class and meet in the cafeteria.

The student leaders were there but had no time to devise a plan to handle the unruly group in front of them. One took it upon himself to take the microphone. I don't remember his exact words, but he calmed the group and acknowledged their anger, an anger he shared. Someone suggested a walkout. He agreed but told students not to do it if they just wanted an excuse to miss class. He implored them to be serious, that the situation demanded it. He sounded far older than his years. He led the walkout: hundreds of students left class to march outside the school, peacefully. When it was over, students returned to class.

When staff saw who was leading the march many were aghast. Some were angry. They felt he shouldn't be trusted; he wasn't the right kind of student for such responsibility. He had a reputation that placed him firmly in the "negative leader" category. Complaints came to administrators. His actions, and therefore those of the program, were dangerous.

Others began voicing their concern that the student leaders were out of class too often. They had to miss eight days a year to prepare and conduct the quarterly meetings. Some teachers said the meetings were a waste of time—all students did was talk. We countered this assumption by inviting teachers to spend a day with us. We only asked that they would stay the entire five hours so they would see the progression, not drop in for a moment and hear something they could consider inappropriate. The principal agreed to provide substitute teachers for those who wanted to attend, but only a handful ever made it to the meetings. We had always made it known to students that if they led or attended a meeting, it was their responsibility to complete the classwork they missed, but some teachers started refusing to let students leave, telling us that what was going on in their class was just too important to excuse them. Many said they worried all this race talk only made things worse.

I think many of the teachers were right. The program was dangerous—it empowered students to think, talk, listen, and act responsibly for themselves. It modeled a new concept of shared power between adults and students. The old paradigm with adults in authority seemed safer. Each year, the funds that provided us release time from our own teaching schedules, to be able to travel to other schools, to provide food for the meetings diminished. There was pressure for the program to end.

Besides, all those black and white students did was talk.

Perhaps some teachers recalled their own futile conversations to close the achievement gap. I see the difference. In contrast to adults, most students came to the meetings willing to examine their own strongly held beliefs, even to suspend them long enough to consider a view posed by someone different from themselves. They still had the flexibility of mind to admit when they might have been wrong. And they were often willing to change not only their mind but also their behavior in small but significant ways.

They were hungry to learn. Many teachers had never seen that appetite in their own classrooms.

When you decide to really listen to someone, you grant them power. There is no power shift from listener to speaker. No one loses. No one is diminished. Both benefit. When the listening is reciprocated, both have an opportunity to learn.

A Tenet of Shared Power: Curiosity

My favorite title is not *educator.* It's *grandmother.* The job is exhausting. At three years of age, my first granddaughter counters nearly every statement I make with, "Why?"

"The dog is barking." *Why is he barking Gam?*

"It's snowing." *Why is it snowing?*

"What a pretty night." *Where's the moon, Gam?*

It never ends. Nearing her first birthday, granddaughter number two spends all waking moments engrossed in science experiments. Grabbing whatever is within her reach, from a toy to a crumb of food on the floor, she examines and then tastes it. It is her scientific method to discover the world. I have to be vigilant. Her experiments are bold and sometimes dangerous. When she grabs the electric cord, I need to intervene. Both girls live in what appears to be an innate and permanent state of curiosity. In his recent book *Curious: The Desire to Know and Why Your Future Depends On It,* Ian Leslie cites the work of professor Paul Harris and psychologist Michelle Chouinard, who report that "between the ages of two and five, children ask a total of forty thousand explanatory questions."[91] Questions are crucial to cognitive development. What happens to the questions, to curiosity, as children turn into teens and adults? Leslie writes:

> A school is a crucible of curiosity. It can imbue young children's fledgling desire to learn with strength and

> sinew, or it can be the place where it is allowed to atrophy.[92]

When curiosity dies, learning dies with it. Ian Leslie criticizes our current schools, stating:

> Our educational system is increasingly focused on preparing students for specific jobs. To teach someone to be an engineer or a lawyer or a programmer is not the same as teaching them to be a curious learner—yet the people who make the best engineers, lawyers, and programmers tend to be the most curious learners. So we find ourselves stuck in a self-defeating cycle: we ask schools to focus on preparing students for the world of work rather than on inspiring them, and we end up with uninspired students and mediocre professionals.[93]

A 2004 Gallup Youth Survey asked middle and high school students to describe how they felt in school, and sadly, it supported Leslie's assertions. Far from educators' lofty goal of empowered learners, students described themselves most often as "bored" and "tired."[94] In a more recent study, students repeated "bored," "tired," with the addition of "stressed."[95] Many educators might describe themselves in the same manner. We think we are teaching our subject area, but what we model is what students learn. A teacher's boredom, exhaustion, and anxiety are contagious.

The demands of teaching and the lack of respect for the profession in our country have left teachers depleted. I once had a student from India whose parents came to school to thank me for educating their daughter. They said, "In our culture, teachers are next to God." I'm not sure who I'm standing next to in America, but it's no one divine. Little money and less prestige, it's easy to forget the passion for learning that brought you to the classroom. Educators must continue to model and ignite education's essential art of questioning. When both teacher and student are allowed to question, the classroom becomes an active place of shared power. Perhaps this is where some educators struggle. If we dispense knowledge only through lectures and note taking, we keep students passive, silent, and controlled. Educators can't predict where students' open inquiry will lead. Classrooms come alive. If we actually believe in empowering students, we must encourage their questions, even when we don't have any answers.

We need curious students because we need curious adults.

Ian Leslie tells us "Curiosity is unruly."[96] We, in The Land of Only White, like order. The system that allows us to hold the most power could crumble if we questioned it. Remember Truman living unaware in the elaborately constructed television set? His elementary school teachers taught him that the world had already been completely discovered. There was nothing left to explore. For a long time he believed them and remained captive. It wasn't until he became curious enough to question his world that he was able to break free. Remember Ben, who constructed the social web of his friends? His curiosity allowed him to question where his prejudice had come from. And the CRD Program defied a school's institutional message that they should be separated by race, curious enough to listen and learn from each other. I think we adults need to take a lesson from children or, as in my case, grandchildren.

TWO TENETS OF SHARED POWER: LAUGHTER AND SORROW

LAUGHTER IS A TEACHER'S SURVIVAL TOOL. No wealth or fame in this profession, just a lot of hard work. If you aren't having some fun, it's just not worth it. If you don't hear yourself laugh out loud with joy now and then, find a new job. But laughter is more than a teacher's way to stay sane. It is a powerful tool for establishing trust, even when all else has failed.

Malik had been my student for about two weeks; conflict and distrust defined our relationship. My every request determined that he would do the opposite, loudly. Even when I asked him to leave class, he refused. Anger was our mutual response to one another, but laughter broke our pattern.

It was a Friday, and both teacher and students were glad for the end of the week. A vocabulary test stood in the way of the weekend. To make it a bit more fun, I had decided to ask students to act out certain words. They would then have to write whether the portrayal clearly defined the word or fell short. Their response had to include one way the act could have been improved to more clearly illustrate the word. The first was *apathy*. A student volunteered to demonstrate the word, walked up to the front and collapsed into a chair. He sunk low into the seat, closed his eyes, and sighed deeply.

Then he muttered, "School is so boring; I just don't want to do anything." Students nodded, and began writing.

And so the test continued. But the day before Malik and I had devised a plan to alter the exam. After class, I had pulled him aside. He was eying me suspiciously. I quickly continued while I had his attention. "One of the words on the test tomorrow is *defiant.* In the middle of the test, when I look out the window, I want you to do your thing.'"

"What does that mean?" he asked with distain.

"I want you to tell me off. I want you to get loud, and tell me you aren't taking this stupid test anymore. I think you should throw in a couple swear words."

"Really?" He looked genuinely interested.

"Yes, and then I'm going to yell at you, and throw you out. When you leave, tip over your chair, slam the door. When you're out, I'll turn and say calmly to the students, 'Did Malik act defiantly? Write out a detailed answer.' Then I'll signal you to come back in. Will you do it?"

Before he agreed, he wanted clarification. "May I really swear?" Malik had been swearing at me on a regular basis; now he was asking permission.

"Yes," I said with confidence.

Malik and I shared our first smile, and then we both laughed.

The next morning, Malik, who was habitually late for class, was sitting in his seat before the bell. He couldn't wait to start the test. When I gazed out the window, he erupted right on cue, and students looked stunned. One begged him, "Chill out, dude," but Malik kept right on rolling, surpassing my request with more than a couple of swear words.

With the slamming of the door, every eye turned to me, and when I said "Question #4: Did Malik act 'defiant?' Explain your answer" there was a dumbfounded silence. As Malik entered with a grin; the students exploded in laughter.

Malik and I never had a problem again.

And we educators need to remember to laugh at ourselves occasionally too.

The school was in the midst of a lock-down drill. These are the days of Columbine and Sandy Hook, so while everyone knew it was a drill, there was still an undercurrent of anxiety. In the dark classroom, students sat in silence, backs against the wall, away from the glass in the door and from a potential shooter's sites. One student whispered to me, "What would you do if a gunman busted in on us?"

All eyes starred me down. "I'd save you," I said with quiet certainty. "I'd stand up to him." Looking at my teenage students, I saw only little children.

The next day, teaching in front of the classroom, I saw the quick dart of a mouse scurrying in sheer panic across the linoleum floor, getting lost in the maze of desks. I matched his fear, screaming and jumping up on a chair. Several six-foot boys joined me. A girl, who remained seated, said with utter disgust, "It's only a mouse."

I responded to the whole class, "You know how I said I'd save you from a gunman yesterday? I wouldn't count on it." We all laughed.

I think back to Jawanza Kunjufu's belief that a teacher must bond with students before real learning can occur. In the first few weeks of each new school year, there is a kind of tension as we try to figure each other out. I know the bond is forming the first time we laugh together. Laughter confirms community. I was once told that some Native Americans have a special ceremony to celebrate a child's first laugh, signifying that the child belongs not only to the spirit world but has now joined the earthly realm also. Laughter levels the playing field and unites us as equals in our humanity.

Sorrow unifies also. Remember Bryan Stevenson's book *Just Mercy*, the one so painful to read I considered quitting? Thank goodness I didn't because near the end he quotes writer Thomas Merton:

> We are bodies of broken bones. I guess I'd always known but never fully considered that being broken is what makes us human. We all have our reasons. Sometimes we're fractured by the choices we make; sometimes we're shattered by things we would never have chosen. But our brokenness is also the source of our common humanity, the basis for our shared search for comfort, meaning, and healing. Our shared vulnerability and imperfection nurtures and sustains our capacity for compassion.[97]

Bryan Stevenson reflects, concluding, "We have a choice. We can embrace our humanness, which means embracing our broken natures and the compassion that remains our best hope for healing. Or we can deny our brokenness, forswear compassion, and, as a result, deny our own humanity."[98]

Sometimes, when teaching symbolism, I tell students we are going to play the modeling game. First, I ask students to list five or six people that have made a serious impact on their life, for good or for bad. I do the same. One at a time, those who choose to do so will pick students to represent these people, placing them in various positions to symbolize the impact they have had. Students always look confused, so I demonstrate. I use a male student to stand with his back to my back, and then three female students are chosen. One girl I place quite close to me, one a bit farther away but still close enough that we can touch hands, and one kneels down in front of me. Finally, I choose one other male to stand on a chair behind me with his hand on my shoulder. I then explain the symbolic significance of my model. The male standing back to back with me is my husband. We have each other's back. Students laugh, understanding the placement. The girls represent my daughters, one very close to me who is my first-born; the second my most independent daughter although we are still very much connected, and the last on her knees represents my baby. Even though she's fully grown, I wish I could keep her small. Students nod, some saying that's how their moms feel about them. But they most want to know about the male on the chair. Who is he and why is he up there? I tell them, "That's my brother who died when I was seven. I always feel he's protecting me from above, in heaven." The class goes silent. Many understand. Loss unites us.

Students ask to show their models. I am always amazed by their honesty and willingness to share their pain. They put students in the hall and close the door on them to represent fathers who walked out of their lives or are in prison. They gather chairs around them and put students on them to signify those they have lost through death. And when the bell rings signally the end of class, no one bolts for the door. Students often tell me after this day, "It just kind of feels like we're family."

Families share laughter and tears. We are reminded of our commonality. Too often our country seeks division by class, race, religion, or gender. Defined by our differences, we forget the simple joys and sorrows that link us: the birth of a child, the loss of a loved one, the security of belonging, the pain of loneliness. Laughter and tears dissolve barriers. We share the powerful bond of humanity.

A Tenet of Shared Power: Finding Purpose

THE SCHOOL'S BASKETBALL COACH and I share many of the same students. We meet often, and the conversations usually conclude that whether you teach on the court or coach in the classroom, our roles mirror one another's. One thing I know for sure: when it's basketball season, the achievement gap narrows. Students have to maintain their grades to be eligible to play. Those I have not been able to reach suddenly come alive in the classroom. Academics and attendance matter. Being a member of the team has a motivating power like no other. When a player's grades are low, the team is on that student, supporting and expecting more. They share a common purpose that unites them beyond their race or economic level.

Martin Luther King Jr. wrote, "Power properly understood is nothing but the ability to achieve purpose."[99] The basketball players have a common purpose, motivating them on the court and in the classroom. They are my shining examples of shared power, diminishing none but empowering all.

Martin Haberman describes ineffectual classrooms as places where the roles of teacher and student are distinctly different. In this model, "Teaching is what teachers do.

Learning is what students do."[100] The teacher is seen as the expert, the student as passive recipient. This can foster a *me* and *them* mentality that often ignites conflicts and a struggle for power. When teacher and students see themselves as members of a learning community, responsibility for the classroom's well-being is shared also. Conflicts lessen and the need for discipline diminishes as students are invested in a partnership they trust values them. When groups share power and purpose, achievement is possible.

All I could see of Frederick were his dreadlocks draped over his desk. His face was buried into his arms, but I could see his pencil moving. This did not look like the appropriate position for proper note taking, and my lecture was fascinating. I was describing the amazing images of Paul Laurence Dunbar's poem "We Wear the Mask."[101] The mask itself, the "torn and bleeding hearts," the smile that hides the cries from "tortured souls"—and Frederick's position never changed. This was Frederick's typical position during class, and I assumed he was bored, wasting time once again, doodling without even considering the poem's power. I began to swoop down on him. This time, I would straighten this young man out. I would make him pay attention and learn.

Frederick could sense my presence, and for a second he buried himself deeper into his arms, but the pencil continued to move. When my hand touched his shoulder, he uncoiled and revealed his paper. The most amazing artwork met my gaze. All of the Dunbar's creations were there, the pencil lines growing dark and bold around the mask itself, which split in half, opening to reveal behind it a bleeding and broken heart. A woman holding a baby looked toward heaven, the look on her face clearly depicting the tortured soul within.

I lost my words, and my lecture stopped. Preparing to reprimand, now I was silenced by the creative intelligence I saw displayed. "Continue," I whispered. I returned to my mechanical words.

After class, I stopped Frederick. He had stuffed the work into his backpack. I asked him for it, and at first, he hesitated. I think he still expected to hear a rebuke for not taking notes in the appropriate Cornell Note form. I waited till all the other students had left the room and then spread the crumpled paper onto my desk.

"My I have this?" I asked. "May it be a part of the quiz tomorrow?" Frederick looked shocked.

"What? You want it?"

"Yes, I want them to analyze it, to tell me how it relates to the poem. I want students to write about your work."

Frederick beamed but took the paper back. "I'll get it to you by the end of the day. I want to finish it, to make it better."

He turned to leave with his artwork in his hand but stopped at the door. "Will I have to write about it also?"

"No," I said. "Clearly, you understand the poem deeply."

Frederick smiled.

After that, Frederick always had his artwork as a part of each test. Students analyzed his artistic portrayal of each literary work we studied. He had found purpose in class. And in recognizing his strengths, I learned more about the literature I thought I knew.

I am sure what is true in the classroom could also be true in our country. When Frederick found his purpose, he had value, and the entire class benefitted, but I could have overlooked his talents. I could have trusted my first mistaken assumption of his disinterest and dismissed him. How often in The Land of Only White do our stereotypes blind us from seeing the strengths in one another? And in contrast to the basketball team's shared purpose, we have no Team America. In The Land of Only White we use the terms of *us* and *them* when referring to our fellow citizens. Remember the students all balancing on one chair, working to support each other? Remember the Kellogg Foundation's findings that racial divisions deplete us all but in reform, we would prosper? We need leadership that works to dismantle the current system of division, replacing it with policies that encourage all to find and achieve their own individual purpose, unified to work towards America's greatest potential.

A Tenet of Shared Power: Dignity

"By any means necessary." Malcolm's most infamous phrase. Taken out of context, the words were often perceived as a violent threat against white America. Put them back, and you will hear Malcolm's actual demand:

> We declare our right on this earth to be a man, to be a human being, to be respected as a human being, to be given the rights of a human being in this society, on this earth, in this day, which we intend to bring into existence by any means necessary.[102]

Far from a call to arms, Malcolm's demand was dignity for all. American playwright Arthur Miller defined dignity as, "Finding your place in the world as a person of worth."[103] A fellow educator refers to this definition when he talks of teachers being in "the dignity business." I think this is what sharing power means to me in the classroom and beyond its walls in my own life: trying to see people for who they are and who they can become, acknowledging the dignity or potential dignity each possess.

English teachers cherish stories. We believe they have the power to educate. It's why when we stand in a library we feel the timeless presence of authors who speak their truth. We want to share these stories with our students. Now I realize each of the students who sit before me have their own story that can educate me. I think of an old African proverb: "When an elder dies, it's like a library burning." But you don't have to be old to have a story. Each of us is a walking text, a volume of our life's chapters. Often within those pages of our existence, we find our dignity. We want others to know our story, just as my students want to share theirs. Remember my first rule, to read critically? I'd like to adjust it, to read the stories of others, being critical of yourself to withhold judgment. Listen to the stories of others; be curious to hear the joys and sorrows that define them; make this our common purpose. In this act, we share power and dignity.

Malcolm X stares at me every day from the poster that hangs in my classroom. His hand is up, his finger pointed in my direction. In his countenance I used to see only a black man's anger that I had been taught to fear. Now I see a man who holds me accountable for educating all children, regardless of race. He commands me to live up to the dignity the title *educator* requires. So many students sit before us, convinced of whom they are: the unwanted, the unrecognized, the unintelligent, the fearful. *By any means necessary*, I must ensure they develop their true abilities to succeed, to be smart, to make choices for their futures. They may not believe they are capable of this when they begin the year, but they must experience it to some degree before they leave my class. For some, it will only be momentary flashes of their true potential; for others they will transform. And this is not because I am a magician. It is because I stand with Plato when he said power is innately in them already.[104] My job is to provide experiences for them to become acquainted with their power. And for those students who already live their power, I must get out of their way. Good little white girls raised in The Land of Only White weren't allowed to demand anything. Malcolm helped me grow up. Now I demand this of myself as an educator.

Thirty-five years into my career, I feel I have earned the right to demand something of my fellow educators also. If you chose this profession, bring honor to it. Lives depend on it. I once met a teacher who had been a commander in the Coast Guard before entering the classroom. He told me of the ships he helped save, the harrowing rescues he had been a part of. "No one ever drowned on my watch," he said with pride. "But now in my classroom, students are drowning all around me, and I don't know how to save them." He teaches with the passion the craft demands. Rather than blaming those who are sinking, he holds himself accountable for their lives. By any means necessary, we must fight against any form of education that diminishes a student and wage war against the achievement gap.

Sharing power is possible in classrooms; I believe it is possible in our country as well if we realize we are all educators of someone. Classrooms are constructed around each of us; our words and actions instruct others, whether we intend it or not. We educate in our homes, neighborhoods, churches, and places of work. We educate others not only when we demand attention, but just as much when we think no one is watching. Each of us must ask the question "What is my life teaching the world?"[105]

Whatever the lessons, take responsibility for them. It may seem an impossibility to right the wrongs of America's system of injustice, but individuals, in the ways they choose to conduct themselves in the smallness of daily life, have the power to chip away at it.

To my fellow constituents raised in The Land of Only White, for all I have learned, I am still one of you. I have no right to demand anything because I am still struggling to free myself from the boundaries that blind us all. But I implore us to address the hypocrisies we choose to ignore. You don't have to agree with me on the issues of race I write about, but I ask you to bring them into the light of evaluation and honest debate. I say there is a system of racism still thriving in America. What facts will you bring to refute me?

Malcolm X attempted to free African Americans from their self-doubt and despair over a society that didn't want them. He told them to stand and be powerful. And then he told all of us, regardless of race, to do the same. This should be our common purpose. Malcolm despised the system of oppression in our country that confers power to some and denies it to others. He wanted power to be shared and respected those who stood up to fight for it. What could be more American that individual power and freedom?

Members of my own extended family ask me what it is that I want. They think I might be ashamed of being white. They think I commit the same sin of generalizing about them as I feel they do of others.

I am not ashamed of being white; I'm ashamed that I thought I was better.

And when I speak of The Land of Only White I write only of those who choose to live apart from others, whether it be a conscious decision or one so buried they no longer feel its presence. They think I want them to give money to welfare programs and handouts to the poor. I do not.

Malcolm X instructed African Americans to "wake up, clean up, stand up, and once we can stand up like a man on our own feet, we stop begging the white man."[106] He did not want alms. Neither do I. Ironically, it's not what I want them to do; it's what I want them to stop doing. There is just one thing: Stop teaching racism.

Stop the comments at the dinner table that reveal disdain for others and affirm their superiority; forget the *harmless* jokes they tell, which their children both laugh at and learn from; stop the derogatory language that goes unchecked. I want them to break the generational cycle of racism they teach to their children.

And for my own children? Their lives might have been easier if I had never met Malcolm X. Now, I teach them the ritual of questioning. I want them to question everything, and that includes me. I don't want charm school books on their heads; I want them to read and listen and learn from all—and trust their own brains to, as Malcolm believed, learn to think for themselves.

I do demand they discover who they were meant to be. Not my expectations, but their own, because they are capable of greatness. I don't have to agree with the decisions they make. I only want to know they made them from positions of power and dignity. Then they must speak their truth.

A PILGRIMAGE

BOTH PLATO AND MALCOLM BELIEVED in a journey, one that each person must travel for himself. For Plato, it was an allegorical ascension out of a cave from ignorance to enlightenment. For Malcolm X, it was an actual physical journey: the pilgrimage to Mecca required of every Muslim once in a lifetime. I have experienced both. Having walked thousands of miles in classrooms without going anywhere, metaphorically, I have traveled far from the land of my beginning. I'm not enlightened, but at least I know now how much I don't understand. As far as a physical pilgrimage, New York City became my Mecca in 2001.

The morning of September 11, 2001, found me where I have spent most of my adult life, in a classroom. My husband called shortly after the first plane had crashed into the World Trade Center. He began with the words, "I think I am watching the worst thing in my life."

I told other teachers what was occurring. Soon we were all riveted around televisions in our respective classrooms. I watched the faces of my students as much as I watched the screen. When the second plane hit, when the towers collapsed, when we heard another plane had crashed into the Pentagon, I felt my age in a classroom of youth. I knew we would go to war and wondered which students it would claim.

A month later New York Mayor Giuliani implored Americans to come to his city saying:

> If you were planning to come to New York sometime in the future, come here now. Come to enjoy our thousands of restaurants, the museums and sporting events and shopping and Broadway; but also come to take a stand against terrorism.[107]

We would go. My husband and I planned a trip over the upcoming Thanksgiving break. We would pack up our three daughters and drive through the night to New York City. We would do as Mayor Giuliani asked: go to a play, eat in the restaurants, see the Statue of Liberty. We would tell our children not to be afraid even if we were. And we would go to Ground Zero.

New York City was crowded and noisy; Ground Zero was crowded and hushed. The ghostly gray smoke still rose from the tangled metal, all that was left of the World Trade Center. Watching through my children's eyes, I knew this sight would stay with them forever. They would tell their children.

Just as Malcolm's pilgrimage to Mecca allowed his vision to expand beyond the constraints of black and white, for a while, the atrocity of 9/11 improved our sight. We remembered we were a nation of diversity, unified as Americans.

But it didn't last. Fear blinded us again. There was a backlash against Arabs and Muslims living here, the majority American citizens themselves. We have a right to fear terrorism and a responsibility to fight it. But what should frighten us even more is when our fear leads to sweeping generalities of any group. After 9/11, too many of us succumbed to our anxieties by demonizing Muslims and Arabs instead of acknowledging the dangers of a faction of Islamic terrorists. Why didn't we fear all Christians and all white people when the KKK terrorized our country? The KKK members saw themselves as good Christian Protestants acting in accordance with their faith. When terrorists look like us, it seems easier to keep generalizations in check. Clearly, most of us do not see ourselves in the fanaticism of the KKK. But if the skin color and religion are not our own, if they represent an *other*, it is much easier for fear to cloud reason.

After 9/11, one of my own family members told me, "It really isn't the blacks we have to fear anymore; it's those Muslims." A fellow teacher told me she was very worried that President Obama might be in league with the terrorists. When I asked her why, she replied, "Well, his middle name is Hussein, a common Muslim name." This was the reasoning of an educator based not on knowledge but on fear.

It was then that the full impact of my pilgrimage to New York City came into focus. Initially, I had seen only in one-dimensional white. When I crossed the hall, I began to see color. Race and racism, the strength of diversity, and the ugliness of division came into consciousness. I began to consider all the ways, even beyond race, that we who were raised in The Land of Only White attempt to isolate ourselves from what we perceive to be others. Over thirty-five years, thousands of students have come through my classroom door. Each one has offered to be my teacher if I only listen. Those who resemble me have a story worth telling and worth hearing, but when someone is an other to me, whether by race, religion, gender identity—any difference—the potential for learning is increased.

I had seen Mathew, a white student, in the hallways of my high school. He steered his motorized wheel chair through the halls like a master. Obviously, he had been confined to it for a very long time, maneuvering the halls with ease. But it made me uncomfortable to look at him. He sat crumpled in the chair, bent in unnatural places. While his hand remained steady on the controls, his body moved spastically. His head was tilted at an odd angle, looking up. I didn't meet his eyes. His adult aid followed behind him, bumping into students as he tried to follow through the crowded halls.

Then I got the news that the following semester, Mathew would be in my class. I tried to ignore my fears, telling myself he would be just another student who I would, of course, treat like anyone else. But Mathew was different, an other to me. His cerebral palsy not only contorted his body, it caused severe and painful cramping of his muscles. I was told that some days his condition might require his aid to remove him from his chair, place him on the floor, and stretch his limbs to relieve the pain. I just couldn't figure out what to do with this information. Should I stop class and wait till he was ready again for the lesson to continue? Should I ignore and proceed? I couldn't figure it out, so I blocked it out of my mind and waited for his first day in class.

It came and passed without incident. He didn't need to be removed from his chair. In the whole semester, it only happened twice, and by then, Mathew had told me not to worry. I should just go on teaching.

Mathew told me a lot that I needed to hear. He told me quite loudly.

He had been in class several weeks when he raised his hand to speak. Calling on him, he said quite clearly, "Fuck you." His speech often was affected by his condition. He stuttered, his breath coming irregularly when he spoke. But "Fuck you" was very, very clear.

All of us in class heard it. When I reflected later, I realized I had somehow come to the conclusion that people in wheelchairs didn't swear—that they were passive people who never got angry. I'm not sure how I came to this conclusion, but clearly it was inaccurate. My interactions with people in wheel chairs was almost nonexistent. I didn't hear them at all. But I heard Mathew.

I asked him to follow me into the hall. There I bent over and asked in my kindest voice, "What's wrong?" And he told me. He said every day I bent over when speaking to him, using a sickeningly pathetic voice I reserved only for him, as if I was just so very, very sorry for him. And in that piteous voice, I would tell him, "That's okay, Mathew, you don't need to do the homework." "That's okay, Mathew, you don't need to come to my desk. I'll come to you." "That's okay, Mathew, you don't need to do..." I told him repeatedly and with confidence that he was less than the *normal* students.

And now he told me I was wrong.

That conversation took awhile. He was very upset. He stuttered and gasped to get this message out. But it wasn't just the cerebral palsy that attempted to rob him of his voice. Everyday, I robbed him even more of his dignity. Finally, I was listening. I heard every word. And he was right about it all.

Before this young man, I had never confronted my fear and discomfort of those who have disabilities. Like pretending not to see color, I said I didn't notice the disability—that of course I treated everyone the same. Mathew helped me see a part of myself I didn't want to acknowledge. When that conversation ended, the secure image I had of myself as a fair person was dismantled. I was truly lost.

"Amazing Grace," the haunting hymn by John Newton, has followed me my whole life. I remember it in church as a child and at my father's funeral as an adult. I chose it to be sung at my wedding and hope my children play it at my funeral. It is only recently that I have learned its origins.

John Newton was a slave trader whose conversion to Christianity ultimately led him to renounce his profession. But he didn't have an immediate epiphany of slavery's injustice as I would have wanted to believe. It took him almost a lifetime, some thirty-four years, before he publically stated, "It will always be a subject of humiliating reflection to me, that I was once an active instrument in a business at which my heart now shudders."[108] He may have written, " 'Twas blind, but now I see,"[109] but in truth, his sight came slowly.

I could say I have found my vision, and that I am no longer lost, but it would be a lie. My eyes are still clearing. Playwright Edward Albee wrote, "Sometimes a person has to go a very long distance out of his way to come back a short distance correctly."[110] Just as John Newton, it has taken me some thirty-four years to understand the actual distance between my two classrooms, between white people and black people in America, and to realize that there is more that divides us than only race. I'm still wandering in the hallway, still in need of my guides. Different from John Newton, I do not believe I have been found. Instead, I am content with being lost and continuing to search.

PAROLED

THIRTY-FIVE YEARS SERVED, and I am free. Retired. But just like the recidivism of so many prisoners, I couldn't stay away from this institution. I found a way to return to schools as an educational consultant. I now work for WestEd, a non-profit, public research, and development agency located in San Francisco, California; the program I am affiliated with is titled *Reading Apprenticeship*.[111] It's the second word *apprenticeship* that captured me. The interdisciplinary program asks teachers to reflect on their practice, to redefine their role. Instead of being the giver of knowledge, educators are asked to see themselves as artists who apprentice students into the craft of reading and thinking critically within their subject area. Reading Apprenticeship honors the bond of shared power between teacher and student, challenging teachers to "become the guide on the side, not the sage on the stage."

Reading Apprenticeship provides the tools to empower students to become independent readers and critical thinkers. I think of Malcolm's words: "The most important thing we can do today is learn to think for ourselves." I no longer see his face every day on the poster in my classroom, but his message permeates this work. And when I think about what it will take to destroy the Achievement Gap, literacy emerges as the central element. Reading Apprenticeship wages war on the Achievement Gap.

Now, instead of my single classroom, I am allowed into classrooms across the country. I work with hundreds of educators who battle each day against ever-increasing odds for their students' survival. The problematic parallels I saw between my classroom and my country are still present; in fact, they are magnified. We remain a nation divided.

I work in a school where all the students are Hispanic and live in poverty. When I tell the cab driver, a Hispanic gentleman, where I need to go, he says, "What? You don't want to go there. It's not a safe place." His face still reflects his concern when we arrive at the school's entrance. He asks me the exact time I will be finished working for the day, assuring me he will be the one to pick me up on time. He will get me out of this neighborhood safely. I work there for three days, and always he is the one to escort me, even though his shift has ended.

In this school district, teachers are frustrated. They believe improving the literacy of their students could empower these students, but there are no books and no library. Those who mandate policy made the decision to go paperless. Each student has been given a computer. These teachers and their students knew what those who made the decision did not: in this neighborhood, the computers would be stolen on the walk home from school. Now students have neither books nor computers. They do not have the literacy skills needed to change the future they see determined for them. This school resides in the shadows of some of the wealthiest communities in America where books, libraries, and home computers are taken for granted. As a colleague once eloquently stated, "Reading, and its role in promoting achievement, is fundamentally an equity issue."[112] There is no equity here.

I work in another school across the country, but the cab driver's reaction is even more extreme. When I tell him the school's address, he says, "You shouldn't be there, day or night. It isn't safe." When he drops me off, he repeats himself, "Look, you just aren't safe. I'll watch you get inside, but I won't come back. Cab drivers don't want to come here." While the school itself appears strong and secure, the neighborhood homes are worn and gray, many boarded up. Black men stand on front steps, looking lost.

As I enter the building, I can't help consider the toll this environment takes on students. I want students to become powerful thinkers who can determine their own lives, but I wonder how much the very necessary thoughts of survival shackle them?

As if to wake me from my revere of despair, a little African American boy runs up to me as soon as I'm in the building. He doesn't know I'm not a teacher here. White and old, I look like one, so he beams up at me, asking, "Did my football jersey get here?" The resilience of youth. At what point does it die?

I find I have learned a lot about the reality of our country from cab drivers. They do not paint the deceptive picture of fairness and equality I used to hold. They don't live in shadows but in stark reality. To one driver, I question him about all the adults I see on street corners. They all wear yellow, reflective vests. He explains, "Those are parents of the students who go to school here. They volunteer to make sure their kids get safely to the building and back home at night. The neighborhood just isn't good. You'll see them in the morning and late afternoon each day." My reaction is a strange mixture of deep respect for the parents and utter despair that children in America need this kind of protection. One of my colleagues went to school in a wealthy suburb just miles from this school. His parents didn't own yellow vests. The divides in our country run deep.

In another high school whose students are predominantly black and live in poverty, teachers attacked the achievement gap directly with their own hands. They served breakfast to students who live daily with hunger. Before standardized tests that can determine educational futures, they cooked pancakes, poured cups of orange juice, and talked with students about the importance of being prepared mentally and physically to do their best. I applauded their efforts. They were, however, forced to stop. Testing officials said unless every student in every class in every district was served breakfast, their actions gave these students an unfair advantage. Breakfast was deemed an inequitable edge for these students while the disadvantages of poverty and hunger were ignored. These teachers tried another less obvious tactic. Having heard the benefits of peppermint to support memory and mental function, students were offered a peppermint candy before the test. Again, they were rebuked and told to stop—the injustice of peppermint candy but not systemic poverty.

In another town that ranks as one of the poorest in the country, poverty and crime have taken their toll. A teacher tells me of a student who sits with a bullet still in his abdomen, of others that have been lost to violence. He tells me that students struggle to see the value in education when their futures seem determined already. Attendance is sporadic. I ask what most students do after high school. "Some get out and go to college, but too many of my female students end up pregnant, hope to get married in the future, and struggle to find work. For the males, some see a future career in a factory or the military. For others, prison ends future plans." Yet he continues to fight for students to envision and achieve more.

In this school I observe a teacher whose classroom poses challenges I never encountered nor could have imagined. Near the back of the room sit two males totally disengaged from the lesson. They huddle over cell phones and laugh out loud at private jokes. The teacher asks them repeatedly for their attention, to put the phones away. They laugh at her also. Another student continually interrupts the lesson to report the two males are breaking the "no cell phone rule." Across the room a girl mumbles to herself and another is completely silent.

After class, the teacher tells me about her daily challenges. The two young men are gang members. They often threaten the student who reports they are breaking rules. He is autistic and doesn't perceive the danger. The girl who mumbles is schizophrenic and is literally in conversation with the voices she hears. When she takes her medication she has better days, but medication costs money, and her mother struggles to provide. The silent girl has just come to the country and speaks almost no English. This teacher has no aids, is clearly exhausted, and yet tells me, "They are all very bright…I just keep trying to reach them."

Public perception of teachers is often one of indifference or disapproval. People say they are overpaid for the work they do, that benefits and pension should be slashed, that they don't even work a full year. This perception is not the reality I encounter. I see silent warriors who, in the face of ever-increasing odds, preserve, protect, and propel students toward a better future. They try to build relationships in the face of ever increasing class sizes. They try to differentiate instruction while the range of abilities within a single class grows. They try to be creative without time for reflection. They face students who bring the complex problems of their existence into the classrooms with them but are without school counselors or social workers. They try to raise families with a paycheck that can't cover the cost of living and find second jobs in the summer to supplement their income. One teacher tells me, "If educators could just make the same money as the city's firemen, I'd be happy." I can't help but think how similar firefighters and teachers are: both attempting to save lives as the environment burns down around them.

Two statements made by educators who teach far across the country from one another remain with me. The first said in apologetic honesty, "I don't have time to teach students to think." His worth as an educator is now determined by the results of the standardized test his students are mandated to take at the end of the year. He tells me, "The test doesn't evaluate thinking. It measures your ability to memorize facts. I know I should be teaching them to think; that's my job as an educator, but I've got to cover all this information to get them ready for the test." He is on a mission he doesn't believe in, but his salary, his job itself, and his ability to provide for his family depend on what students bubble in for a correct answer. Thinking has to go.

The other, whose students live in abject poverty, struggles to motivate them to see the power of education. The idea of academics allowing them more choice in their future is too abstract for them. The students see little relevance in school and learning itself. She tells me, "Curiosity has died in them."

These two teachers and their students do not live in The Land of Only White, yet we who do often suffer from the same ills. We aren't thinking, and we aren't curious. As Ian Leslie writes, "A policy of deliberate ignorance is often adopted by those who wish to protect their own power."[113] He continues, quoting psychologist Daniel Kahneman, "Our comforting conviction the world makes sense rests on a secure foundation: our almost unlimited ability to ignore our ignorance."[114] Curiosity would make us wonder about what sustains the disparity between ourselves and others. Thinking would fuel the questions needed to reform the system of inequality that exists in our country.

I have two questions. The first: *Why does the Achievement Gap still exist?* It lived within my classroom for thirty-five years. I know it existed before that and continues unabated. *Why?* There are the complex issues we openly discuss: racial, social, and economic factors that intertwine, making its destruction difficult. But now I consider another reason: perhaps we in The Land of Only White don't want the achievement gap to disappear. It's a needed cog in the system that protects our position and power. I think back to my principal's repeated question to her teachers: *Do you really believe all kids can learn?* It was so easy to answer yes. So much more work to really examine what exists beneath the surface of a quick response. Do we really want to empower all students or only some? Empowered students of color would do more than close the achievement gap; they would dismantle the system that favors us.

I think most in The Land of Only White are cognizant that the public school system is filled with inequities. We know some students receive a better education than others, and our children are the ones who benefit. We literally just don't see the children who live with less. While we can't be blamed for what we don't see, we can't keep choosing blindness. What does it reveal about our hand in the design when we spend more tax dollars building and maintaining prisons than for improving public schools? Poor schools begin the pathway to prison. Both institutions work to keep our land colorless.

My second question is for all who were raised or remain in The Land of Only White. *Do we want to share our land with others?* Fifty years ago The Kerner Report told America that unless it addressed the racism at its core, our country would divide into a white and black America. The warning has become reality, but it's a white and *others* divide. Currently, there is a proposal to construct a wall to keep out illegal immigrants from Mexico, a ban on Muslims entering our country, and a cry to deny refugees seeking safety on our soil. Still we profess, "Diversity makes us stronger." Which message, a wall or a welcome, do we extend to others?

I recently worked in school with a large Arab and Muslim population. A white friend asked me if I was going there to "straighten them out." When I asked what he meant, he said confidently, "Well, you know. The way they treat women, the way they make them dress. The way they act. How violent they are. You need to bring some sense to them." I was working on improving literacy rates. "Straightening them out" was not on my agenda, but it was on his. He wanted *them* to learn to act like us, or keep away. Build that wall whose foundation is fear.

In contrast, a white teacher shared with me that many of her Hispanic students worry about their families being deported. Anxiety consumes them, making it difficult to focus on academics. When I observed her classroom the next day, I saw this for myself. Students were discussing *To Kill A Mockingbird.* I noticed one student with her head down. Midway through the lesson her hand went up. She was crying and struggled to get her words out. "Am I going to have to leave the country?"

Without hesitation, this teacher confidently replied, "You aren't going anywhere. If I have to, I'll adopt you. I don't have a lot of money, so we'll both have to work, but we'll be fine."

Another student blurted out "Is there a limit to how many of us you can adopt?" Clearly this teacher believes in sharing her classroom, country, even her home.

I think of two rules for recess posted in an urban elementary school. "Don't go outside the fence. Don't talk to anyone outside the fence." Designed to protect these children, they reflect The Land of Only White's own unwritten but understood edicts to keep us safe.

So how do we answer: *Do we want others to live in our land?* If the answer is no, *why?* What informs this conviction? The reality is The Land of Only White is shrinking. But if the answer is yes, what must change? I remain convinced that America must adopt a new paradigm of shared power. And I am just as sure education—both in classrooms, in interaction with others, and in critical self-reflection—can facilitate this change.

I have listened and learned from those who raised me in

The Land of Only White. Since leaving its borders I've just had to reevaluate the lessons. Some of the teachings just aren't true. We do see color and racism isn't over. But I certainly still honor the tenets of hard work and self-reliance. People need to take responsibility for themselves. I recently came across the following quote I think might capture the sentiments of many in The Land of Only White:

> The black man never can be become independent and recognized as a human being who is truly equal with other human beings until he has what they have, and until he is doing for himself what others are doing for themselves. The black man in the ghettoes, for instance, has to start self-correcting his own material, moral and spiritual defects and evils. The black man needs to start his own program to get rid of drunkenness, drug addiction, prostitution. The black man in America has to lift up his own sense of values.[115]

Surely, the author of these words would be welcomed to sit at our table, but if I tell you they are the words of a black Islamic leader, would it change your ability to listen? Would Malcolm X still be allowed a seat?

If I had remained in The Land of Only White, I would have met Plato but not Malcolm X. Malcolm X gave me a new understanding of my country, my classroom, and even my own family. He helped me understand Plato's wisdom. Both men have helped me move beyond the borders of my understanding. The highest accolade of my career came from a student. She said, "You took our minds and handed them to us, and made us think for ourselves. You helped us use the voices we'd always had, but were too afraid to use."[116] She got it wrong. She and all my students, the colleagues of my past and those I work with today, and of course Plato and Malcolm X, they all educated me. They gave me my mind back. They gave me my voice. I'm not afraid anymore.

I have been a teacher for so long I have watched my students age. Many stay in touch and allow me to share the joys of a wedding and the birth of a child. I have attended college graduations and watched students enter careers in education, in medicine, in politics. I believe in youth and in the adults they become.

Perhaps, after all, education is the nondenominational church I have been searching for. All belong, even the atheist just looking for a place to sit. It is a sanctuary and the ritual is, as Ta-Nehisi Coates said, to constantly question. Malcolm X stated in the year before his death, "Education is an important element in the struggle for human rights. It is the means to help our children and our people rediscover their identity and thereby increase their self respect."[117] When there is mutual respect, there is shared power.

One final memory: My sister used to collect dirt in tiny pill bottles. She kept them in a drawer, and I remember peering in to study them. Her goal was to gather the earth from all fifty states. Each was labeled precisely. Too young to read, I saw the varied hues contained in each: the reds of the Dakotas, the deep browns and blacks of Tennessee, the pale sands of California. The colors didn't mix. At some point she threw them all away.

I like to imagine them somewhere, bottles cracked and dirt

pouring out into one massive pile of soil. Something could take root in it, could grow. Separated in their sterile containers, there was no chance of life, but now…

Kind of like in Plato's cave, I imagine myself somewhere buried beneath that dirt, looking for light. I'm trying to dig myself out, trying to unearth all the lessons on race, all the education of exclusion, I was taught. I'm trying to unlearn them and see for myself. Every now and again, I get a glimpse of the sun.

THIS BOOK IS FOR the woman who, as a child, remembers going to church each Sunday with her family. She also remembers her little white robe complete with the little white hood, just like her father's. She remembers standing under the light of the KKK's burning cross.

When her mother died, she told me the men with the white robes came. They left their hoods off. They marched in formation to the cemetery behind her mother's casket. They helped bury her. And she buried the secret she begged me not to tell. Now that she is dead and gone, I offer it up. Offered not in shame, but in the power of redemption, in the light of healing.

I honor this woman who succeeded in unlearning much of the racism of her past. We all need to keep trying. I think it is a lifelong attempt.

NOTES

1. Plato, "The Simile of the Cave" *The Republic*, Book VII, 514a-c to 521a-e trans. Grube (London: Penquin Books, 1992)

2. George F. Root, "Jesus Loves the Little Children" 1864.

3. Richard Wright, "The Man Who Killed a Shadow," *Eight Men*, (New York: Harper Perenial, 1961.

4. Martin Luther King, Jr., "I Have a Dream," March on Washington, 1963, 5.

5. Ozzie Davis, Eyes on the Prize II Interviews, 1989.

6. Plato, Plato's Apology, (38a5-6).

7. Oppression, https://en.wikipedia.org/w/index.php?title=Oppression&oldid=820118889.

8. Michelle Alexander, *The New Jim Crow: Mass Incarceration in the Age of Colorblindess* (New York: The New Press, 2010), 184.

9. Institutional racism, https://en.wikipedia.org/w/index.php?title=Oppression&oldid=820118889.

10. Kenneth Clark, Doll Test Harlem New York (Gordon Parks, 1947)

11. Kira Davis, A Girl Like Me, 2005.

12. Anderson Cooper, Study: White and black children bias toward lighter skin, CNN, 2010.

13. Margaret Beal, Study: Study, CNN, 2010.

14. Malcolm X, https://www.goodreads.com/quotes/460913-america-s-greatest-crime-against-the-black-man-was-not-slavery.

15. Joseph Goebbels, Publications Relating to Various Aspects of Communism (1946) United States Congress, House Committee on Un-American Activities, Issue 1-15, 9.

16. Alexander, *The New Jim Crow.*

17. Gary Orfield and Chungmei Lee, Historic Reversals, Accelerating Resegregation, and the Need for New Integration Strategies, Civil Rights Project UCLA, 2007.

18. Malcolm X, "Mascot," *The Autobiography of Malcolm X as told to Alex Haley*, (New York: The Ballentine Publishing Group, 1964), 38.

19. Malcolm X, "Out," *The Autobiography of Malcolm X*, 318.

20. Nathan McCall. "Dispatches from a Dying Generation." Washington Post, January 13, 1991.

21. Signithia Fordham and John Ogbu, "Black Students' School Success: Coping with the 'Burden of Acting White'", *Urban Review*, Vol. 18, 1986, 176-206.

22. Kujufu p.

23. "Race Against Time: Educating Black Boys," NEA, Feb. 2011.

24. 2011 United States Justice Report.

25. Malcolm X, "Nightmare," *The Autobiography of Malcolm X*, 22.

26. Plato, "The Simile of the Cave" *The Republic*, Book VII, 514a-c to 521a-e trans. Grube (London: Penquin Books, 1992) p. 257.

27. Malcolm X, Harlem Rally on the White Man, speech, 1963.

28. Robert Rosenthal and Lenore Jacobson, Urban Rev (1968) 3:16. https://doi.org/10.1007/BF02322211.

29. Dr. Beverly Tatum, *Why Are All the Black Kids Sitting Together in the Cafeteria?*(New York: Basic Books), 1997, 6.

30. Anderson Cooper, Study: White and black children bias toward lighter skin, CNN, 2010.

31. Peggy McIntosh, "White Privilege: Unpacking the Invisible Knapsack," Peace and Freedom Magazine, July/August, 1989, 10-12.

32. Jane Elliot, http://www.newsreel.org/transcripts/essenblue.htm.

33. Devah Pager, "Study: Black man and white felon-same chances for hire," Princeton University, 2008.

34. Tracy Jan, "White families have nearly 10 times the net worth of black families. And the gap is growing," The Washington Post, September 28, 2017.

35. Tami Luhby, "The black-white economic divide in 5 charts," CNN Money, 2015.

36. Plato, "The Simile of the Cave," 256.

37. F. Scott Fitzgerald, "Rich Boy," Short Stories of F. Scott Fitzgerald,(New York: Simon and Schuster, 1989) 318.

38. Plato, "The Simile of the Cave," 257-258.

39. Jonah Lehrer, "Don't: The Secret of Self-Control," The New Yorker, May 18, 2009.

40. Langston Hughes, "Harlem," 1951.

41. Rachel E. Morgan, "Race and Hispanic Origin of Victims and Offenders 2012-2015," Bureau of Justice Statistics.

42. Nathan McCall, "Dispatches from a Dying Generation."

43. Malcolm X, Speech at the Founding Rally for Afro-American Unity, 1964.

44. Eric Gunwald, "Step 4: Revise," The Writing Process, Massachusetts Institute of Technology. https://writingprocess.mit.edu/process/step-4-revise.

45. Lisa Delprit, *Other People's Children: Cultural Conflict in the Classroom*, (New York: The New Press), 2013, 55.

46. Malcolm X, The Autobiography of Malcolm X, 120.

47. Louis Lomax, A Summing Up: Louis Lomax Interviews Malcolm X, 1963.

48. Plato, "The Simile of the Cave," 257.

49. Ani Turner, "The Business Case for Racial Equality," W.F. Kellogg Foundation, 2015. 5.

50. Ani Turner, "The Business Case for Racial Equality," 7.

51. Ani Turner, "The Business Case for Racial Equality," 13.

52. U.S. Census Date and Vera Institute of Justice, 2012.

53. U.S. Census. 2010.

54. Alexander, *The New Jim Crow*, 7.

55. Alexander, *The New Jim Crow*, 6.

56. Alexander, *The New Jim Crow*, 100.

57. Alexander, *The New Jim Crow*, 7.
58. Malcolm X, *The Autobiography of Malcolm X*, 416.
59. Malcolm X, "Letter to the Egyptian Gazette," 1964.
60. Abraham Lincoln, "First Inaugural Address," 1861.
61. E.M. Forrester, "Tolerance," *Two Cheers for Democracy*, 1951.
62. Malcolm X, *The Autobiography of Malcolm X*, 120.
63. Mark Twain, The Adventures of Huckleberry Finn, (New York: Penguin Books), 1884, 169.
64. Mark Twain, Notebook, 1895.
65. Leon Festinger, *Psychologists on Psychology*, (New York: Taylor and Francis), 1977, 104.
66. Ta-Nehisi Coates, *Between the World and Me* (New York: Spiegel & Grau, 2015).
67. Journalism in the Digital Age, "The Echo Chamber Effect." https://cs181journalism2015.weebly.com/the-echo-chamber-effect.html.
68. Ozzie Davis, Eulogy for Malcolm X, 1965.
69. Cass R. Sunstein and Reid Hastie, " 'Happy Talk' and the Dangers of Groupthink," Time, January 14, 2015.
70. Stanley Cohen, *States of Denial: Knowing about Atrocities and Suffering*, (Cambridge: Polity Press), 2001.
71. Malcolm X, *The Autobiography of Malcolm X*, 176.
72. Adler Mortimir, "How to Mark a Book," The Saturday Review of Literature, July 6, 1941.

73. Coates, *Between the World and Me*, 52.

74. Coates, *Between the World and Me*, 27.

75. 11 Facts about Literacy in America, DoSomething.org https://www.dosomething.org/us/facts/11-facts-about-literacy-america.

76. "The US Illiteracy Rate Hasn't Changed in 10 Years," Huffington Post, September 6, 2013.

77. Frederick Douglas.

78. Malcolm X, "To Mississippi Youth," 1964.

79. Huron High School, Ann Arbor Public Schools, https://www.a2schools.org/Domain/1688.

80. Plato, "The Simile of the Cave," 256.

81. William Shakespeare, "The Tragedy of Macbeth," The Riverside Shakespeare, (Boston: Houghton Mifflin Company,) 1974, 1329.

82. William Shakespeare, "The Tragedy of Macbeth," 1312.

83. Langston Hughes, "Coffee Break," *Tales of Simple*, 1965.

84. George Orwell, Animal Farm (New York: Harcourt, Brace and Company), 1946, Chapter 10.

85. Plato, "The Simile of the Cave," 264.

86. *, Creating Cultures of Thinking: The 8 Forces We Must Master to Truly Transform Our Schools, (Jossey-Bass: San Francisco), 2015, 25.*

87. Martin Haberman, "The Pedagogy of Poverty Versus Good Teaching," 1991.

88. Jawanza Kunjufu, 100 Plus Educational Strategies to Teach Children of Color, (New York: African American Images), 2008.

89. Carol Dweck, *"Stanford University's Carol Dweck on the Growth Mindset and Education". OneDublin.org. 2012-06-19.*

90. Stephanie Siek and Joe Sterling, "Census: Fewer white babies being born," CNN, May 17, 2012.

91. Ian Leslie, *Curious: The Desire to Know and Why Your Life Depends On It*, (New York: Basic Books, 2014), 28.

92. Leslie, *Curious*, 108.

93. Leslie, *Curious*, xxii.

94. Linda Lyons, "Most Teens Associate School with Boredom, Fatigue," Gallop News, June 8, 2004.

95. Catherine Robertson Souter, New England Psychologist, January 1, 2016.

96. Leslie, *Curious*, xiv.

97. Bryan Stevenson, *Just Mercy: A Story of Justice and Redemption* (New York: Spiegel & Grau, 2015), 289.

98. Stevenson, *Just Mercy*, 289.

99. Martin Luther King, Jr., "Where do we go from here?" Southern Christian Leadership Conference, August 16, 1967.

100. Martin Haberman, The Pedagogy of Poverty Versus Good Teaching, 1991.

101. Martin Luther King, Jr., "Where Do We Go From Here?" Southern Christian Leadership Conference. August 16, 1967.

102. Malcolm X, Speech at the Founding Rally for the Organization of Afro-American Unity, June 28, 1964.

103. Arthur Miller, "The American Writer: The American Theater." Speech at University of Michigan Hopwood Awards, 1981.

104. Plato, "The Simile of the Cave," 261.

105. Robby Novak. "Pep Talk for Teachers and Students." https://www.youtube.com/watch?v=RwlhUcSGqgs.

106. Malcolm X, "Wake Up, Clean Up, Stand Up," https://www.youtube.com/watch?v=z5JEhmrJcJs.

107. Rudy Giuliani, Addressing the United Nations, New York Times, October 1, 2001.

108. John Newton, "Thoughts Upon the Slave Trade," John Newton, 1788.

109. John Newton, "Amazing Grace," 1779.

110. Edward Albee, "The Zoo Story," (New York: A Signet Book), 1959, 21.

111. Reading Apprenticeship at WestEd, https://readingapprenticeship.org.

112. Bill Loyd, Reading for Understanding, (Jossey-Bass: San Francisco), 2012, 3.

113. Ian Leslie, *Curious*, 101.

114. Ian Leslie, *Curious*, 40.

115. Malcolm X, *The Autobiography of Malcolm X*, 281.

116. ChyAnne McKinney-Thomas, "Letter to Ms. Why," Talking Back/Giving Thanks, (Ann Arbor: 820Michigan & Blotch Books), 2010, 132.

117. Malcolm X, Speech at the Founding Rally for the Organization of Afro-American Unity, June 28, 1964.

BIBLIOGRAPHY

Alexander, Michelle. "Legal Scholar: Jim Crow Still Exists in America." NPR, "Fresh Air," with Terry Gross. https://www.npr.org/2012/01/16/1145175694/legal-scholar-Jim-crow-still-exists-in-america.

Alexander, Michelle. *The New Jim Crow: Incarceration in the Age of Colorblindness*. New York: The New York Press, 2010.

Albee, Edward. *The Zoo Story*. New York: A Signet Book, 1959.

Clark, Kenneth. "Doll Test Harlem New York." Gordon Parks, 1947. http://www.loc.gov/pictures/item/95505330.

Coates, Ta-Nehisi. *Between the World and Me*. New York: Spiegel & Grau, 2015.

Cohen, Stanley. *States of Denial: Knowing about Atrocities and Suffering*. Cambridge: Polity Press, 2001.

Cooper, Anderson. "White and Black Children Bias Toward Lighter Skin." CNN, 2010. http://www.cnn.com/2010/US/05/13/doll.study/index.html.

Davis, Kira. "A Girl Like Me," 2005. https://www.youtube.com/watch?v=EivX77ORIIs.

Davis, Ozzie. "Eyes on the Prize II Interviews." Interview by Madison Davis Lacy, Jr. 1989. http://digital.wustl.edu/e/eii/eiiweb/dav5427.0777.037ossiedavis.html.

Davis, Ozzie. "Eulogy for Malcolm X," 1965. http://malcolmx.com/eulogy/.

Delprit, Lisa. *Other People's Children: Cultural Conflict in the Classroom.* New York: The New Press, 2013.

Do Something.org. "11 Facts about Literacy in America." www.dosomething.org/us/facts/11-facts-about-literacy-america.

Douglas, Frederick. https://en.wikiquote.org/wiki/Talk:Frederick_Douglass.

Dweck, Carol. "Stanford University's Carol Dweck on the Growth Mindset and Education." OneDublin.org. 2012-06-19.

Elliot, Jane. California Newsreel, 1999. http://www.newsreel.org/transcripts/essenblue.htm.

Festinger, Leon. Psychologists on Psychology. New York: Taylor and Francis, 1977.

Fitzgerald, F. Scott. *Short Stories of F. Scott Fitzgerald.* New York: Simon and Schuster, 1989.

Fordham, Signithia and John Ogbu. "Black Students'School Success: Coping with the 'Burden of Acting White.'" Urban Review, Vol. 18, 1986.

Forrester, E.M. "Tolerance," Two Cheers for Democracy, 1951. http://emforster.de/hypertext/template.php3?t=tc.

Giuliani, Rudy. Speech addressing the United Nations, New York Times, October 1, 2001.

Goebbels, Joesph. Publications Relating to Various Aspects of Communism (1946), United States Congress, House Committee on Un-American Activities, Issue 1-15, 9.

Greenleaf, Cynthia and Ruth Schoenbach. *Reading for Understanding.* San Francisco: Jossey-Bass, 2012.

Gunwald, Eric. "Step 4: Revise." The Writing Process, Massachusetts Institute of Technology. https://writing.process.mit.edu/process/step-4-revise.

Haberman, Martin. "The Pedagogy of Poverty Versus Good Teaching." Phi Delta Kappan, v73 n$ p290-94 Dec. 1991. https://eric.ed.gov/?id=EJ435783.

Hastie, Reid and Cass R. Sunstein. " 'Happy Talk' and the Dangers of Groupthink." Time, January 14, 2015.

Huffington Post. "The US Illiteracy Rate Hasn't Changed in 10 Years." September 6, 2013 https://www.huffingtonpost.com/2013/09/06/illiteracy-rate_n_3880355.html.

Hughes, Langston. "Coffee Break," Tales of Simple, 1965. http://routes-mag.com/langston-hughes1965-tales-of-simple-coffee-break/.

Hughes, Langston. "Harlem." Montage of a Dream Deferred. New York: Henry Holt and Company. 1951.

Huron High School, Ann Arbor Public Schools. https://www.a2schools.org/Domain/1688.

Jacobson, Lenore and Robert Rosenthal. Urban Rev, 1968, 3:16 https://doi.org/10.1007/BF02322211.

Jan, Tracy. "White Families Have Nearly 10 Times the New Worth of Black Families. And the Gap is Growing." The Washington Post, September 28, 2017.

Journalism in the Digital Age, "The Echo Chamber Effect." https://cs181journalism2015.weebly.com/the-echo-chamber-effect.html.

King Jr., Martin Luther. "I Have a Dream," speech at the March on Washington. August 28, 1963. https://www.archives.gov/files/press/exhibits/dream-speech.pdf.

King Jr., Martin Luther. "Where Do We Go from Here?" speech at Southern Conference, August 16, 1967. http://www-personal.umich.edu/~gmarkus/MLK_WhereDoWeGo.pdf.

Kunjufu, Jawanza. *100 Plus Educational Strategies to Teach Children of Color.* New York: African American Images, 2008.

Lee, Chungmei and Orfield, Garyand.

Lehrer, Jonah. "Don't: The Secret of Self-Control." The New Yorker, May 18, 2009.

Leslie, Ian. *Curious: The Desire to Know and Why Your Life Depends On It.* New York: Basic Books, 2014.

Lincoln, Abraham. "First Inaugural Address," 1861. http://avalon.law.yale.edu/19th_century/lincoln1.asp.

Loyd, William. *Reading for Understanding.* San Francisco: Jossey-Bass, 2012.

Luhby, Tami. "The Black-White Economic Divide in 5 Charts." CNN Money, 2015. http://money.cnn.com/2015/11/24/news/economy/blacks-whites-inequality/index.html.

Lyons, Linda. "Most Teens Associate School with Boredom, Fatigue," Gallop News, June 8, 2004.

McCall, Nathan. "Dispatches from a Dying Generation." Washington Post, January 13, 1991.

McKinney-Thomas, ChyAnne. "Letter to Ms. Why," Talking Back/Giving Thanks. Ann Arbor: 820 Michigan & Blotch Books, 2010.

McIntosh, Peggy. "White Privilege: Unpacking the Invisible Knapsack." Peace and Freedom Magazine, July/August, 1989.

Miller, Arthur. "The American Writer: The American Theater." Speech at University of Michigan Hopwood Awards, 1981.

Morgan, Rachel E. "Race and Hispanic Origin of Victims and Offenders 2012-2015." Bureau of Justice Statistics. https://www.bjs.gov/content/pub/pdf/rhovo1215.pdf.

Mortimir, Adler. "How to Mark a Book," The Saturday Review of Literature, July 6, 1941.

Newton, John. "Amazing Grace," 1779.

Newton, John. "Thoughts Upon the Slave Trade," 1788. https://www.biblestudytools.com/classics/newton-posthumous-works/thoughts-upon-the-african-slave-trade.html.

Novak, Robby. "Kid President's Pep Talk to Teachers and Students." https://www.youtube.com/watch?v=RwlhUcSGqgs.

Orfield, Gary and Chungmei Lee. "Accelerating Resegregation, and the Need for New Integration Strategies," Civil Rights Project UCLA, 2007.

Orwell, George. *Animal Farm.* New York: Harcourt, Brace, and Company, 1946.

Pager, Devah. "Study: Black Man and White Felon-Same Chances for Hire." Princeton University, 2008.

Plato, "Plato's Apology," (38a5-6). https://www.theguardian.com/theguardian/2005/may/12/features11.g24.

Plato, "The Simile of the Cave," The Republic, Book VII, 514a-cto 521 a-e trans. Grube. London: Penquin Books, 1992.

Ritchhart, Ron. *Creating Cultures of Thinking: The 8 Forces We Must Master to Truly Transform Our Schools.* San Francisco: Jossey-Bass, 2015.

Root, George. "Jesus Loves the Little Children." 1864.

Sered, Danielle. "Young Men of Color and the Other Side of Harm." Vera Institute of Justice, December, 2014.

Shakespeare, William. "The Tragedy of Macbeth." *The Riverside Shakespeare*, Boston: Houghton Mifflin Company, 1974.

Siek, Stephanie and Joe Sterling. "Census: Fewer White Babies Being Born," CNN, May 17, 2012. http://inamerica.blogs.cnn.com/2012/05/17/census-2011-data-confirm-trend-of-population-diversity.

Souter, Catherine Robertson. New England Psychologist, January 1, 2016.

Spencer, Margaret Beale. "White and Black Children Bias Toward Lighter Skin." CNN, 2010. http://www.cnn.com/2010/US/05/13/doll.study/index.html.

Stevenson, Bryan. *Just Mercy: A Story of Justice and Redemption.* New York: Spiegel & Grau, 2015.

Tatum, Beverley. *Why Are All the Black Kids Sitting Together in the Cafeteria?* New York: Basic Books, 1997.

Turner, Ani. "The Business Case for Racial Equality," W. F. Kellogg Foundation, 2015. https://www.wkkf.org/resource-directory/resource/2013/10/the-business-case-for-racial-equity.

Twain, Mark. *The Adventures of Huckleberry Finn.* New York: Penguin Books, 1884.

Twain, Mark. Notebook #35, 1861. http://www.twainquotes.com/Huckleberry_Finn.html.

US Census Data and the Vera Institute of Justice. "Education vs Prison Costs," 2015. https://prisoneducation.com/prison-education-news/t6fplu6p683cqfcv8beqrh2syflyoi.

Wikipedia contributors, Oppression. https://en.wikipedia.org/w/index.php?title=Oppression&oldid=837247976.

Wright, Richard. "The Man Who Killed a Shadow." *Eight Men.* New York: Harper Perenial, 1961.

X, Malcolm. *The Autobiography of Malcolm X as told to Alex Haley*. New York: The Ballentine Publishing Group, 1964.

X, Malcolm. Harlem Rally on the White Man speech, 1963. https://www.youtube.com/watch?v=xMHzLFmMfRw.

X, Malcolm. https://www.goodreads.com/quotes/460913-america-s-greatest-crime-against-the-black-man-was-not-slavery.

X, Malcolm. "Speech at the Founding Rally for Afro-American Unity," 1964. http://www.blackpast.org/1964-malcolm-x-s-speech-founding-rally-organization-afro-American-unity.

X, Malcolm. "Letter to the Egyptian Gazette," 1964. http://malcolmxfiles.blogspot.com/2013/07/letter-to-egyptian-gazette-august-25.html.

X, Malcolm. "A Summing Up: Louis Lomax Interviews Malcolm X," 1963. http://teachingamericanhistory.org/library/document/a-summing-up-louis-lomax-interviews-malcolm-x.

X, Malcolm. "Wake Up, Clean Up, Stand Up." https://www.youtube.com/watch?v=z5JEhmrJcJs.

www.ingramcontent.com/pod-product-compliance
Lightning Source LLC
Chambersburg PA
CBHW020252030426
42336CB00010B/729

* 9 7 8 1 7 3 3 7 8 1 0 0 8 *